access t

PHILIP II

David McKinnon-Bell

Hodder & Stoughton

A MEMBER OF THE HODDER HEADLINE GROUP

Acknowledgements

The author wishes to thank Maria Parker for her assistance in translating Philip II's letter to Don Diego de Chaves Orellana on page 27.

The front cover illustration shows Philip II from San Lorenzo Reale de El Escorial/Institut Amatller d'Art Hispànic.

The publishers would like to thank the following individuals, institutions and companies for permission to reproduce copyright illustrations in this book: AKG London, pages 60 and 135; AKG London/Erich Lessing, page 50; AKG London/Joseph Martin, page 61; © Bettmann/Corbis, page 49; *Allegory of the Battle of Lepanto* by Titian, Museo del Prado, Madrid/ Institut Amatller d'Art, Hispanic, page 137; *The Adoration of the Name of Jesus* c.1578 by El Greco, The National Gallery, London, page 101.

The publishers would also like to thank the following for permission to reproduce material in this book: The Continuum International Publishing Group Ltd for extracts from *War and Government in Habsburg Spain* by I.A.A. Thompson, Athlone, 1976; HarperCollins Publishers for the extracts from *The Mediterranean in the Age of Philip II*, vol.2 by F. Braudel, Collins, 1973 and pp.85-6 from *The Pursuit of Power: Venetian Ambassadors' Reports* by James C. Davis (editor and translator), English translation copyright © 1970 by James C. Davis, reprinted by permission of HarperCollins Publishers Inc; John Jones for the extracts from *Europe 1500–1600* by J.A.P. Jones, Nelson Thornes, 1997; Longman for the extracts from *Spain 1469–1714: A Society* in Conflict by H. Kamen, Longman, 1991 and *Europe in the Sixteenth Century* by H.G. Koenigsberger and G.L. Mosse, Longman, 1968; Manchester University Press for the extract from *The Spanish Armada* by C. Martin and G. Parker, 1999, imprint 1, Mandolin; The Orion Publishing Group for extracts from *The Spanish Inquisition* by Henry Kamen, Weidenfeld & Nicolson, 2000; extracts from *The Spanish Armada* by Fernandez-Armesto, 1989, © Felipe Fernandez-Armesto 1988, by permission of Oxford University Press; the extracts from *Golden Age Spain* by H. Kamen, Macmillan, 1971 and *Sixteenth Century Europe* by K. Leach, Macmillan, 1980, reproduced with permission of Palgrave; the extract from *Philip II* by G. Woodward, Pearson Education Limited, 1992, reprinted by permission of Pearson Education Limited; the extract from p.98 of *The Adventures of Don Quixote* by Miguel de Cervantes Saavedra, trans. J.M. Cohen, Penguin Classics, New York, 1950, translation copyright © 1950 by J.M. Cohen, reproduced by permission of Penguin Books Ltd; the extracts reproduced from *Phiip of Spain* by Henry Kamen (Copyright © Henry Kamen 1997) by permission of PFD on behalf of Professor Henry Kamen; Thames & Hudson Ltd for the extract from *Philip II* by Pierson; Yale University Press for the extract from *The Grand Strategy of Philip II* by G. Parker, © 1998 by Geoffrey Parker, Yale University Press, 1998;

Every effort has been made to trace and acknowledge ownership of copyright. The publishers will be glad to make suitable arrangements with any copyright holders whom it has not been possible to contact.

Orders: please contact Bookpoint Ltd, 78 Milton Park, Abingdon, Oxon OX14 4SB. Telephone (44) 01235 827720, Fax: (44) 01235 400454. Lines are open from 9.00–6.00, Monday to Saturday, with a 24 hour message answering service. Email address: orders@bookpoint.co.uk

British Library Cataloguing in Publication Data
A catalogue record for this title is available from the British Library

ISBN 0 340 782579

First published 2001
Impression number   10 9 8 7 6 5 4 3 2 1
Year   2007 2006 2005 2004 2003 2002 2001

Copyright © 2001 David McKinnon-Bell

Typeset by Fakenham Photosetting Limited, Fakenham, Norfolk
Printed in Great Britain for Hodder & Stoughton Educational, a division of Hodder Headline Plc, 338 Euston Road, London NW1 3BH by Bath Press Ltd, England.

Contents

Preface

The original *Access to History* series was conceived as a collection of sets of books covering popular chronological periods in British history, together with the histories of other countries, such as France, Germany, Russia and the USA. This arrangement complemented the way in which history has traditionally been taught in sixth forms, colleges and universities. In recent years, however, other ways of dividing up the past have become increasingly popular. In particular, there has been a greater emphasis on studying relatively brief periods in considerable detail and on comparing similar historical phenomena in different countries. These developments have generated a demand for appropriate learning materials, and, in response, two new 'strands' have been added to the main series – *In Depth* and *Themes*. The new volumes build directly on the features that have made *Access to History* so popular.

To the general reader

Access books have been specifically designed to meet the needs of examination students, but they also have much to offer the general reader. The authors are committed to the belief that good history must not only be accurate, up-to-date and scholarly, but also clearly and attractively written. The main body of the text (excluding the Study Guide sections) should therefore form a readable and engaging survey of a topic. Moreover, each author has aimed not merely to provide as clear an explanation as possible of what happened in the past but also to stimulate readers and to challenge them into thinking for themselves about the past and its significance. Thus, although no prior knowledge is expected from the reader, he or she is treated as an intelligent and thinking person throughout. The author tends to share ideas and explore possibilities, instead of delivering so-called 'historical truths' from on high.

To the student reader

It is intended that *Access* books should be used by students studying history at a higher level. Its volumes are all designed to be working texts, which should be reasonably clear on a first reading but which will benefit from re-reading and close study.

To be an effective and successful student, you need to budget your time wisely. Hence you should think carefully about how important the material in a particular book is for you. If you simply need to acquire a general grasp of a topic, the following approach will probably be effective:

1. Read Chapter 1, which should give you an overview of the whole book, and think about its contents.

2. Skim through Chapter 2, paying particular attention to the 'Points to Consider' box and to the 'Key Issue' highlighted at the start of each section. Decide if you need to read the whole chapter.
3. If you do, read the chapter, stopping at the end of every sub-division of the text to make notes.
4. Repeat stage 2 (and stage 3 where appropriate) for the other chapters.

If, however, your course demands a detailed knowledge of the contents of the book, you will need to be correspondingly more thorough. There is no perfect way of studying, and it is particularly worthwhile experimenting with different styles of note-making to find the one that best suits you. Nevertheless the following plan of action is worth trying:

1. Read a whole chapter quickly, preferably at one sitting. Avoid the temptation – which may be very great – to make notes at this stage.
2. Study the diagram at the end of the chapter, ensuring that you understand the general 'shape' of what you have read.
3. Re-read the chapter more slowly, this time taking notes. You may well be amazed at how much more intelligible and straightforward the material seems on a second reading – and your notes will be correspondingly more useful to you when you have to write an essay or revise for an exam. In the long run, reading a chapter twice can, in fact, often save time. Be sure to make your notes in a clear, orderly fashion, and spread them out so that, if necessary, you can later add extra information.
4. The Study Guide sections will be particularly valuable for those taking AS Level, A Level and Higher. Read the advice on essay questions, and do tackle the specimen titles. (Remember that if learning is to be effective, it must be active. No one – alas – has yet devised any substitute for real effort. It is up to you to make up your own mind on the key issues in any topic.)
5. Attempt the source-based questions section. The guidance on tackling these exercises is well worth reading and thinking about.

When you have finished the main chapters, go through the 'Further Reading' section. Remember that no single book can ever do more than introduce a topic, and it is to be hoped that, time permitting, you will want to read more widely. If *Access* books help you to discover just how diverse and fascinating the human past can be, the series will have succeeded in its aim – and you will experience that enthusiasm for the subject which, along with efficient learning, is the hallmark of the best students.

Robert Pearce

1 Philip and the Historians

POINTS TO CONSIDER

This chapter briefly introduces the main historical arguments that have surrounded the character of Philip II through the ages. Look out for the way that contemporaries' and historians' interpretations of Philip's personality reflect their political and religious perspectives.

KEY DATES

1528 Philip born, eldest son of Charles I of Spain (Holy Roman Emperor Charles V).
1540 Philip's mother, Isabella of Portugal dies.
1545 Philip appointed Regent of Spain during his father's absence.
1556 Charles I abdicates and Philip II becomes King of Spain.
1598 Philip II dies.

1 Contemporaries' Views of Philip II

> **KEY ISSUE** Why did contemporaries' views of Philip II differ so widely?

The main issue to be addressed in this book will be the debate over how successfully Philip II governed and preserved the Spanish empire. This has always been a lively contest, since Philip II has always excited controversy and hugely contrasting opinions among historians. To many, he has come to be regarded as Spain's greatest monarch, echoing the plaudits he received from contemporary apologists and official biographers, men like Cabrera de Cordoba, a former courtier and servant of Philip, who regarded the King as the epitome of Royal virtues, and his reign as Spain's 'Golden Age'. His *History Of Philip II, King of Spain* opens with a long exposition of Philip's many talents:

1   In him, as in most princes, was born constancy and a firmness of purpose. Because of his many virtues he was trusted implicitly. Fear neither disturbed nor disquieted him, and he could be trusted with both the conduct of war and the welfare of the state ... His handsome physical
5   appearance, deserving of Empire, was augmented by his dignity, grace and princely demeanour ... He was ever aware of what was going on in his Empire, serving thus as a model for his successors and enabling him to rule his people more wisely ... His astute insights and Providence helped keep his subjects contented; his good judgement enabled him to
10 balance the varying interests of his people and made him flexible in deal-

ing with difficult foreign and domestic problems. ... He was strong in
adversity, restrained in prosperity, and interpreted the Divine in such a
way as to keep his people from superstitious fear.[1]

Philip's Protestant rivals during the second half of the sixteenth century, especially his contemporaries in the Netherlands and England,
took a rather different view of his achievements. Most famously
William of Orange, who led the Dutch Revolt against Spanish rule in
the Netherlands between 1567 and 1584, was bitterly critical. In his
notorious *Apology* of 1581, William of Orange provided perhaps the
definitive statement of the so-called 'Black Legend' of Philippine
Spain, and until recently this coloured much of the historiography of
Philip II in the English-speaking world.

1 Is not this King, who has endeavoured to stigmatise my lawful marriage
   with infamy, the husband of his own niece? ... Does not the voice of
   nature cry aloud against such an incestuous conjunction? And in order
   to make room for this marriage, is it not true that he put to death his
5 former wife, the mother of his children, the daughter and sister of kings
   of France?
      It was not a single murder that was perpetrated for the sake of this
   extraordinary marriage. His son, too, his only son was sacrificed, in
   order to furnish the Pope with a pretext for so unusual a dispensation;
10 which was granted to prevent the Spanish monarchy from being left
   without a male heir. This was the true cause of the death of Don
   Carlos...
      It is against me chiefly that his designs are directed. 'Were I
   removed' he says, 'either by death or banishment, tranquillity would be
15 restored'... There is not, I am persuaded, a nation or prince in Europe,
   by whom it will not be thought dishonourable and barbarous, thus publicly to authorise and encourage murder; except the Spaniards, and
   their King, who have long been estranged from every sentiment of
   honour and humanity. In having recourse to private assassinations
20 against a declared and open enemy, does not this mighty monarch confess his despair of being able to subdue me by force of arms?[2]

2 Historians' Views of Philip II

> **KEY ISSUE** In what ways have historians' views of Philip II
> changed over time?

The Black Legend held sway amongst English-speaking historians
until the twentieth century, and was most forcefully expressed in the
polemical and bitter writing of the American historian, J L Motley:

1 If Philip possessed a single virtue, it has eluded the conscientious
   research of the writer of these pages. If there are vices — as possibly

there are – from which he was exempt, it is because it is not permitted
to human nature to attain perfection, even in evil. The only plausible
5 explanation ... of his infamous career is that the man really believed
himself, not a king, but a God ...

Homicide such as was hardly ever compassed before by one human
being was committed by Philip II when in the famous edict of 1568 he
sentenced every man, woman and child in the Netherlands to death.
10 That the whole of this population, three millions or more, were not
positively destroyed was because no human energy could suffice to exe-
cute the diabolical decree ... Alva, toiling hard, accomplished much of
this murderous work ... and at the end of half a dozen years he could
boast of having strangled, drowned, burned or beheaded somewhat
15 more than eighteen thousand of his fellow creatures.[3]

In the twentieth century, Fernand Braudel's monumental study of the
Mediterranean world in the sixteenth century refocused historians'
attention away from the history of events (*'histoire evenementiale'*), and
onto the 'tides of history', the underlying structures and long-term
developments that, Braudel argued, largely determined the actions of
individual rulers like Philip. Braudel de-emphasised the actions of the
King himself, stressing instead the long-term climatic, geographical
and economic developments, within which policy-makers were
'imprisoned'. According to Braudel, Philip had little influence upon
the ultimate destiny of Spain, and accordingly the debate over the
morality or legitimacy of his actions is, to an extent, a red herring.
Braudel concluded:

1 When I think of the individual, I am always inclined to see him imprisoned within a destiny in which he himself has little hand, fixed in a land-
scape in which the infinite perspectives of the long term stretch into the
distance both behind him and before. In historical analysis as I see it,
5 rightly or wrongly, the long run always wins in the end.[4]

Braudel's analysis of the structures underpinning sixteenth century
life and government led him to conclude that there was little that
Philip II could have done to offset the enormous difficulties inherent
in ruling a huge empire. Consequently, his failure should be seen in
context and the sometimes desperate measures to which he resorted
should be regarded as just that – desperate measures. This evaluation
remains the foundation stone of modern analyses of Philip's reign.

Much of the most recent work on the era has returned to the
person of the monarch, although acknowledging the constraints
upon his actions. Revisionists like Henry Kamen and Geoffrey Parker
point out that the claims of the 'Black Legend' are based on selective
readings of the evidence and the hostile testimony of Philip's rivals.
Several recent studies have offered us a more human Philip, struggling to manage a complex and embattled inheritance with a measure
of success, although Parker is critical of Philip II's foreign policy,
which he characterises as narrowly conceived and ineffective, a failing

which is laid squarely at the King's door.[5] Perhaps most representative of the pro-Philippine school is Henry Kamen, who portrays Philip as a warm and intelligent ruler, unjustly treated by posterity.

> 1 Philip was by temperament tranquil, subdued and always in control of himself ... He lacked neither humour nor vivacity. He enjoyed celebrations, feasts, dances and jousts. He delighted in the outdoor life ... His reserve in speech probably arose from his hyperactive mental
> 5 processes, for his mind had an enormous capacity for storing and using information ... A recurring legend is that of the King's cruelty. No contemporary cites any acceptable evidence for it. As a dispenser of justice he seems to have been rock-hard ... but he restrained the severity of his officials on numberless occasions. As a person he was more gentle.
> 10 He disliked war and violence ... Nowhere in Philip's statements is there any unusual emphasis on the rights of Kings. Like most rulers he was attributed 'absolute power' ... but he did not use the phrase during his reign ... Occasionally, in moments of crisis, he allowed himself to appeal to the traditional right of life and death which a lord could exercise
> 15 over his subjects. He made use of this approach only when there was no obvious alternative ... All the executions known to have taken place during his reign ... were carried out after due legal process and with the participation of the royal council.[6]

Philip II's reign remains controversial, with much to interest the modern student. The difficulties Philip experienced in governing a multiple kingdom, where the only real unifying force was the monarch himself, parallel the problems faced by other rulers in History. Philip grappled with real problems that afflict all governments: dealing with opposition, securing compliance and obedience to the law, educating the people, managing the economy and defending the nation's possessions and interests abroad.

Historians naturally have different perspectives on the question of how effectively Philip coped with his many problems, and the rest of this book will explore some of their conclusions. Whilst you read this book, keep in mind these different perspectives on Philip II. History, (that is the *study* and the *writing* of the past), is constantly under review. Old orthodoxies are challenged and overturned, and in their turn the 'revisionists' become the new establishment, nervously awaiting the broadsides of a new generation of 'revisionists'. Consequently, there is rarely any consensus on a given issue, and 'historical truth' is elusive. The room for manoeuvre that this realisation gives the student of history is half the fun of studying the subject!

References

1 Cabrera de Cordoba, 'Felipe II, Rey de Espana', cited in J. C. Rule & J. J. TePaske, *The Character of Philip II* (Heath, 1963), pp. 4–5.

2 William of Orange, *Apology*, cited in K Leach, *Sixteenth Century Europe* (Macmillan, 1980), p. 75.
3 J. L. Motley, 'History of the United Netherlands', cited in Rule & TePaske, *Character of Philip II*, p. 17.
4 F. Braudel, *The Mediterranean in the Age of Philip II Vol 2* (Collins, 1973), p. 1244.
5 See G. Parker, *The Grand Strategy of Philip II* (Yale, 1998).
6 H. Kamen, *Philip of Spain* (Yale, 1997), pp. 221–8.

Summary Diagram

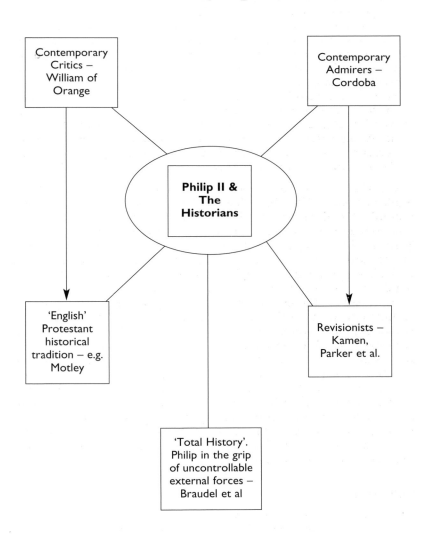

Working on Chapter I

This opening chapter introduces you to a number of contrasting interpretations of the position of Philip II in History. Although at this stage you will not be in a position to evaluate each position and decide which you agree with, you should make **brief** notes on the five main strands of opinion represented above.

In all the note-making that you do at AS and A level, it is important that you are **focused** and **selective**.

1. Before you begin to make notes, you should decide what it is you want to find out. If you don't do so, your notes will lack a structure and you will run the danger of simply re-writing the entire passage out in full.
2. Having decided on the **purpose** of your reading, you should **quickly read** (skim) the whole of the section. This will give you an overview of the **main points. Jot them down**.
3. Now **make brief notes** on the section, using whatever system works well for you. Remember the purpose of notes is to give you something to revise from at a later date. By being concise and selective at this stage of affairs, you are forced to decide what is important and what is not, and this will improve your understanding of the topic. You will also find your notes more manageable when you return to them a few months later.
4. Finally, check back over them. Are they comprehensible and clear? Do they cover the main points that you identified as your purpose at the start?

This sounds like a laborious and slow process, and initially it is, but you should regard note-making as the legwork necessary for you to be able to form historical judgements, engage in debates and write intelligently about historical questions, so it is worth the effort. It will, with practice, become smoother and easier to do, so that eventually you begin to do elements of this process simultaneously. In History, as in everything else, genius is one per cent inspiration and 99 per cent perspiration!

Source-based questions on Chapter I

Source-based questions at A Level may sometimes ask you to evaluate the merits of competing historical explanations. The chapter you have just read includes a number of opinions regarding Philip II. The questions below demand that you pick out significant contrasts and points of comparison between them. Any more sophisticated assessment of the relative merits of these views will require that you have your own knowledge and opinion of the reign, and so this has been left until the conclusion of this book.

1. Three Views Of Philip II

Read the extracts from Cabrera de Cordoba on pages 1–2, William of Orange on page 2 and Henry Kamen on page 4. Then answer the questions that follow.

a) What does William of Orange mean when he refers to 'the death of Don Carlos' (page 2, lines 11–12)? *(3 marks)*

b) Comment on the reliability and usefulness of the accounts given by Cordoba and William of Orange of the character of Philip II. *(5 marks)*

c) Compare William of Orange's account of Philip's character with Henry Kamen's assessment. On what points do they agree and disagree? *(4 marks)*

d) In what ways, and for what reasons, have historians' assessments of Philip II changed since his death? *(8 marks)*

Note that document questions always tell you how many marks are available for each sub-question. This should alert you to the depth and detail required in the answer. Plan the amount of time you spend on each sub-question accordingly. For example, in the questions above, you should aim to spend about twice as long on c) and d) as you do on a) and b). In answering, always take care that you do exactly as requested by the examiner. For example, in question c) above, you will quickly appreciate that the two writers agree on little. Whereas William portrays Philip as a murderer and a ruthless ruler, prepared to use assassination to achieve his political goals, Kamen offers a picture of a cultivated and affable character, even-handed in his administration of justice and scrupulously attentive to the rule of Law. However, they both refer to 'extra-judicial murder', an act of state from which Philip would not flinch if he regarded it as necessary. They refer to different examples, and indeed, William's are invalid, primarily serving a propaganda value to his cause, and lacking a basis in truth. Kamen does not suggest that Philip *never* acted in this way. He offers other cases, however, and stresses the lengths to which the King went to assuage his conscience and legitimise his actions.

Some of the questions above are probably not wholly answerable if you have only read this chapter of the book so far, but return to it when you have finished studying this topic, when you will have the necessary knowledge to discriminate between the relative merits of contrasting interpretations.

2 Philip II's Imperial Inheritance

POINTS TO CONSIDER

Philip II inherited more than half his father's empire and, despite his thorough training, many contemporary and historical commentators have regarded him as temperamentally ill equipped for his arduous role. His 'Spanishness' has been seen as a particular weakness, given the multi-national nature of the empire. Thus, one of the key questions this chapter addresses is 'How well prepared was Philip for the task of ruling the Spanish empire?' Other key issues revolve around the nature and state of the empire he inherited. How unified was the Spanish empire? Was the empire economically and politically healthy at the time of Philip's accession?

KEY DATES

1527	21 May	Philip is born, the eldest son of Charles I (Holy Roman Emperor Charles V).
1543		Charles embarks upon a long series of campaigns in Germany. Philip becomes regent of Spain. He marries Infanta Maria of Portugal.
1545		Philip's eldest son, Don Carlos, is born.
1548-1551		Philip visits Italy, Germany and Flanders.
1554-1556		Philip marries Mary Tudor and spends 2 years in England.
1556	Jan	Charles I abdicates.
	March	Philip becomes King of Spain.

1 Philip's Upbringing and Character

KEY ISSUES How well prepared was Philip for the task of ruling the Spanish empire? How did Philip's character affect his conduct of government?

Philip's birth at Valladolid on 21 May 1527 was an event of the greatest political and dynastic significance. The eldest child of Charles I of Spain, Holy Roman Emperor, Duke of Burgundy and ruler of much of Europe and the New World, Philip's birth guaranteed the succession of the Habsburg dynasty. Yet the Emperor played only a minor role in the upbringing and training of his heir. Charles spent much of Philip's childhood in Central Europe, dealing with the complicated affairs of the Holy Roman Empire and resisting the manifold challenges posed by the Valois Kings of France, the German

Protestant princes, and the Ottoman Sultan, Suleiman. He was away from Spain from 1529 to 1533, and was only intermittently present for the next 10 years. He left Spain again in 1543 and only returned in 1557, having abdicated from the imperial throne. Philip's education was left in the hands of his mother, Isabel of Portugal, and a succession of advisors and tutors.

Probably no ruler in History has enjoyed as thorough a preparation for the throne as Philip II. At the age of seven, he was assigned a tutor, the scholar Juan Martinez de Siliceo, and a governor, Juan de Zuniga. Philip's education included Latin, regarded as essential for any sixteenth century prince, especially one whose dominions included so many different realms speaking such a diverse range of languages. Latin was anyway the language of business, of the Church, of the universities and of diplomacy. However, Philip was no great scholar of languages. His grasp of Latin was adequate, he understood some Portuguese (learned from his mother) but only a little French, and virtually no Italian, German or Flemish, despite his father's determination that he should learn the languages of his subjects. By choice, he spoke only Spanish (and the Castilian dialect at that). Otherwise, his education followed the humanistic fashion of the day, encompassing History, Geography, Greek and Mathematics. He seems to have been a rather reluctant student, preferring to hunt and read the chivalric stories popular with sixteenth century Spanish nobles. Philip was, however, enthusiastic about architecture and natural history, and he acquired a substantial library, including a number of humanist works (many of which he banned later in life). His interest in art led him to patronise some of the greatest painters of the age.

Philip's education became an apprenticeship at an early age. At 12, his mother died, and at the age of 14, he was given his own private secretary, Gonzalo Perez, who served him until his own death in 1566. In 1542, he made his first Royal progress, around Castile and Aragon. The following year, Charles I departed for Germany, leaving Philip, aged 16, behind as regent. Shortly afterwards, Philip married the Infanta Maria of Portugal, further cementing the relationship between the two crowns, only for Maria to die, two years later, in childbirth. Although Philip was closely advised by a clique of hugely experienced men hand picked by his father, he was, from 1543, the effective ruler of the country. These were difficult years for Spain. Charles's wars drained the nation's manpower and finances, and he bombarded Philip with demands for more money. However, the economic boom of the early sixteenth century was gradually slowing to a halt and Philip found the *Cortes* (Castile's parliament) unsympathetic to demands for extra taxation. Gradually, Philip became confident enough to inform Charles, in 1546, that 'we have reached the end of the line. We do not know from where or how to seek ways and means of finding money'.[1] By the time Philip ascended to the throne in his own right, he had outlived the advisors appointed by the emperor and was his own man.

Scholars have traditionally emphasised Charles's influence upon Philip's style of government. On his departure for Germany in 1543, Charles left behind two long, handwritten 'Instructions', full of advice for the young prince on how to conduct himself as Regent. These letters profoundly influenced Philip II's conduct of government over the next 55 years. Charles advised Philip to 'keep God always in mind' and defend the Inquisition. He urged him to uphold justice, tempered with mercy. He should listen to a range of opinions at court, never allowing himself to fall into the possession of one faction or advisor. Philip perhaps followed his father's advice too literally, as he tended to keep information from his ministers, leading to confusion within his government, as more than one minister found that they were working on the same problem, often offering competing advice on the basis of inadequate information. However, although Philip's inability to delegate, a fatal flaw in the ruler of so enormous an empire, may be traced back to an over-liberal interpretation of his father's advice, Philip was temperamentally disinclined to share responsibility too. Charles also cautioned him to take care in conducting his relations with Aragon, whose privileges meant that they were a trickier prospect to manage than Castile. Philip would have done well to take this advice to heart and tread carefully with his more remote possessions, for his reign was to be blighted by a failure to appreciate the perspectives of his provincial subjects. _destroyed_

Notwithstanding Charles's influence, Philip's reign was shaped as much by his own personality. Assessments of Philip's character have, of course, always reflected the prejudices of the historian. Motley's harsh portrayal of Philip II as 'grossly licentious, cruel ... a consummate tyrant'[2] has been moderated by more sympathetic historians, who emphasise his sense of duty, love of justice and attentiveness to his family. The King cultivated a dignified reserve in public, which corresponded to his notions of his appropriate regal dignity. Behind the official mask of formality, Philip was a warm and affectionate husband, brother and father, as his letters to his fourth wife, Ana, and to his daughters Isabel and Catalina, and his respect and admiration for his sisters Maria and Juana all testify. He attended the birth of his children and remained at his wives' side during their illnesses. Contemporaries commented on the way he balanced his familial and monarchical duties.

1   He rises very early and attends to affairs and correspondence until midday, when he eats always at the same time and almost always the same type and amount of food. He drinks from an average size glass, which he drains twice. In general his health is good. However, he some-
5   times suffers from a stomach illness and a bit of gout. Half an hour after lunch, he dispatches all petitions and other documents that need his

signature. Three or four times a week he goes to the country in a carriage, to hunt game and rabbits with a crossbow ... He visits the queen
three times a day; in the morning before mass, during the day before he
10 begins work and at night when he goes to bed. They have two low beds
separated by a palm's width, but because of the curtain covering them
they appear one bed. The king loves his wife deeply and never fails to
visit her.[3]

Historians have frequently criticised Philip for a tendency to procras-
tinate when faced with a decision. He would consult a number of ministers and consider at great length his various options. Was this, as
Cordoba argued, 'prudence' (Philip gained the title 'the Prudent
King' during his lifetime), or was his slow decision-making process
due to weakness of will and sheer indecisiveness, as Pierson has
argued?[4] Philip had a secretary's attention to detail and an autocrat's
desire to know everything that related to the government of his
realms, and this combination was a dangerous mix, since his attempt
to read and notate every document that passed across his desk led to
long hours of paperwork and a tendency to be unable to see the wood
for the trees (see pages 23–7).

Parker argues that this apparent rigidity at key moments during
the reign may have been a product of stress, induced by the onset of
a crisis. Certainly, at times Philip pushed himself to his physical limit;
'I am so busy and deprived of sleep, because I need to spend most of
the night going over the papers that other business prevents me from
seeing in the day'.[5] It appears that Philip took to his bed at particularly stressful times, delaying a decision until he could see which way
events turned. Sometimes, however, these illnesses were genuine, for
his health was always shaky and it deteriorated towards the end of his
reign, the very period of his greatest trials and challenges. When gout
struck, the King's centrality to the machinery of government left it
unable to function. Only in the mid 1590s did he begin to delegate
authority to his son, enabling government to continue when he himself was incapacitated.

Philip was deeply religious, pledged to uphold Catholicism and to
serve God. He attended Mass daily. He had a strong sense of duty,
arguing that 'the community was not created for the prince, but
rather ... the prince for the community'.[6] Possessed of a strong sense
of justice, he once instructed the judge in a case affecting the Crown:
'In case of doubt, the verdict must always go against me'.[7] Perhaps the
best example of his sense of duty was his arrest and detention in 1568
of his only son, Don Carlos, on grounds of insanity and conspiracy
against the crown. Philip never shrank from his monarchical duty.

This did not preclude occasional acts outside the law, carried out
(as he saw it) in the service of the state. Philip was, after all, a product
of the Age of Machiavelli. The arrest, torture and subsequent pursuit
of Antonio Perez (see pages 31–2) might appear to us as the action of

a tyrant with no respect for law, but they were in the King's eyes necessary evils to restore order and peace to the community for which he was responsible.

Philip was, then, a complex individual, capable of great affection, yet cold and calculating towards those who opposed him; cool and dignified in his conduct of public affairs, yet a devotee of hunting and masked balls; religious and devout, yet capable of setting aside both morality and his loyalty to the Pope when it suited him to do so. Judged by the standards of the age he appears neither a tyrant nor an angel.

2 Philip's Inheritance: The Spanish Empire in 1556

> **KEY ISSUES** What was the extent of Philip's empire in 1556? How unified was the Spanish empire? What was the relationship between Spain and its overseas colonies?

When the Holy Roman Emperor Charles V abdicated in 1555–6, he divided his possessions between his brother, Ferdinand, and his son, Philip. Ferdinand received the traditional German lands of the Habsburg family, including Bohemia and Hungary, but Philip took possession of the lion's share of the empire. Thus Spain became the heart of an empire stretching from the Netherlands to the Americas. Philip II's dominions were immense and for that reason essentially ungovernable. Philip was King of Spain, but also separately King of Castile and Aragon, and each of his Spanish kingdoms possessed their own *cortes* (parliament), with which Philip was forced to deal separately when taxation was required. Beyond the peninsula, Philip was also Duke of Milan, King of Naples and Sicily, and ruler of Sardinia. He possessed the strategically vital county of Franche-Comte and his inheritance included the Netherlands, where he was both Duke of Burgundy and separately the ruler of each of the 17 provinces. These diverse provinces were linked in a '*monarquia*' (an extended network of kingdoms) through their acknowledgement of Philip as their ruler, and they emphatically did not regard themselves as part of a 'Spanish Empire'.

The foundations of Philip's *monarquia* lay in the Spanish kingdoms of Castile and Aragon, although these were not wholly unified themselves. Castile, for example, incorporated Granada (conquered in 1492) and Navarra (added in 1515). Granada presented special problems, as more than half of Philip's subjects there were *Moriscos*, former Moslems forcibly converted following the fifteenth century reconquest of the region, but never fully trusted by 'Old Christian' Spaniards. Castile was the linchpin of the monarchy, financial heart of the kingdom and the source of the largest component in Spain's

Spain in 1556

famous *tercios* (the military units of the Spanish army). Although Castile was theoretically a single, unified kingdom with a single *cortes*, the three Basque counties in the North exercised virtual autonomy. Elsewhere in Castile, royal authority was theoretically absolute, but in practice Philip depended upon the great noble landowners to enforce his will and the *Cortes* to raise taxation. The richest of the Spanish kingdoms due to a century of economic growth and the possession of the Indies (which belonged to Castile rather than Spain as a whole), Castile had become dominant in the *monarquia*.

Aragon, the other half of Philip's Spanish inheritance, was a federation of three kingdoms, Catalonia, Aragon and Valencia, each with their own traditions, institutions of government and laws. Whereas Castile's possession of the Indies made it Atlantic-facing, Aragon provided a Mediterranean focus to Philip's Spain, and brought Sardinia and Sicily to the *monarquia*. The great port of Barcelona in Catalonia was the embarkation point for trade to Italy and for Philip's armies en route to central Europe and the Netherlands. Otherwise, Catalonia, which bordered on France, was one of the most vulnerable and lawless regions of Spain, where brigandage was endemic. Royal couriers and bullion shipments ran the constant risk of ambush from bandits as they crossed the Aragonese kingdoms. Valencia, like Granada, contained a significant minority of *Moriscos*, mainly peasant farmers who sheltered from the Inquisition under the protection of their landlords. Across the Mediterranean Valencia faced the pirate states of the Barbary Coast and it was extremely vulnerable to raids. The fiercely defended *fueros* (liberties) of the Aragonese kingdoms made them difficult to govern from Madrid. Philip appointed a viceroy, who governed the kingdom on his behalf, but the powers of his representative were rather limited, and in Aragon the *Justiciar*, invariably a local aristocrat chosen by his peers, wielded great local influence.

Philip's Italian possessions were extensive. Sicily had long been a possession of the crown of Aragon. Naples had been added to the monarchy during the wars against France and, with Sicily, formed the front line of the conflict against the Ottoman Empire. Sicily and Naples were ruled directly by a viceroy (usually a Spaniard), exercising complete authority in Philip's name. Milan was a personal possession of Philip granted to him by Charles V in 1540. The city controlled the wealthy region of Lombardy and was a vital part of the *monarquia*, providing arms, mercenaries and a staging post along the 'Spanish Road' to the Netherlands. Philip's Italian possessions were reluctant to contribute to the finances of the empire unless they could see a benefit directly accruing to them. Thus, the Italian states contributed substantially to the Lepanto campaign against the Turks in 1571, but resisted demands for taxation to finance the wars in the Netherlands.

The most prosperous region of the empire was the Netherlands, but the jealously guarded liberties of the 17 provinces prevented Philip from milking this wealth for the benefit of the empire as a whole. Philip considered the Netherlands an essential part of his inheritance. Philip's father, Charles, had been born there and had counselled his son to guard his possession of these strategically and economically vital lands carefully. However, Philip's attempts to preserve his authority in the Netherlands led to disaster (see pages 45–54). Least remarked upon of Philip's possessions was Franche Comte, but this province possessed immense strategic value. Vitally positioned along the route connecting the Netherlands to Lombardy, the so-called 'Spanish Road', Franche Comte was vulnerable to attack from France or Germany.

Spain's overseas colonial possessions, especially the Indies, were increasingly important to her. By the time of Philip's accession, the major elements of Spain's colonial empire had been established. Aside from the addition of the Portuguese empire (which Philip insisted always remained quite distinct from Spain's colonies), only the Philippines were added (in 1565) to Castile's overseas empire during Philip's reign, although Buenos Aires was settled in 1580. The colonies were a source of great wealth, especially after the famous Potosi silver mines in Peru began production, but their importance required an immense investment in fortifications and galleon

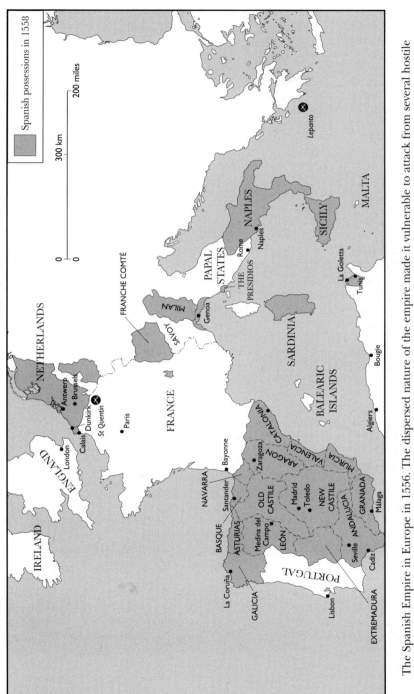

The Spanish Empire in Europe in 1556. The dispersed nature of the empire made it vulnerable to attack from several hostile neighbours.

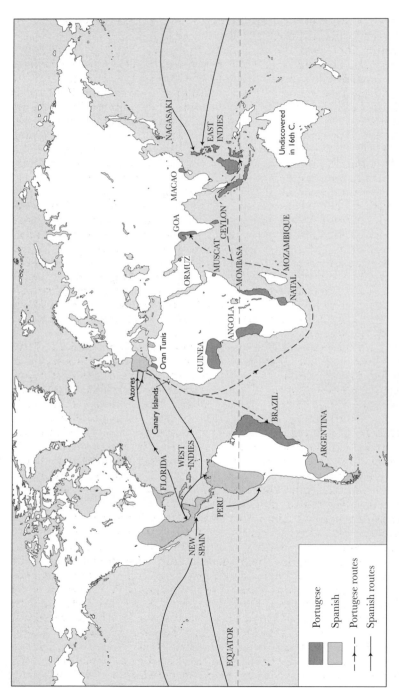

The Spanish and Portuguese Overseas Empires during Philip's Reign. Philip's empire was, as one contemporary observed, the first in *History* on which the sun never set.

EQUATOR

NEW SPAIN

FLORIDA

WEST INDIES

PERU

BRAZIL

ARGENTINA

Azores

Canary Islands

Oran Tunis

GUINEA

ANGOLA

ORMUZ

MUSCAT

MOMBASA

NATAL

MOZAMBIQUE

GOA

MACAO

CEYLON

EAST INDIES

NAGASAKI

Undiscovered in 16th C.

Portugese

Spanish

Portugese routes

Spanish routes

squadrons to protect the Indies and their extended trade routes to and from Spain. Although the acquisition of Portugal's large navy significantly increased the empire's naval capability the Portuguese Empire was enormous, and the defence of Spain's overseas possessions remained extremely difficult. Consequently Drake was able to raid the Caribbean coast almost with impunity during the 1580s.

Governing this far-flung empire presented almost insuperable challenges. Distance made effective communication with Spain extremely slow, and the colonists evolved a semi-autonomous regime, over which Philip's viceroy presided without dominating affairs. In Madrid, the Council of the Indies attempted to keep abreast of developments in the Americas and the Far East, and intermittently (whenever the bullion fleet sailed for New Spain) dispatched orders, instructions and requests for information. Attempts to intervene directly in matters were met with indifference – 'I obey, but do not comply'. Conflicts often surfaced between Spanish-born colonial administrators and the local landowning elite regarding precedence and the implementation of orders sent from Spain, and the solution was usually to arrive at some compromise enabling the colonists to govern their own affairs as they saw fit, whilst respecting (theoretically) the Crown's absolute authority. Given that communication from Spain might be delayed by anything up to 3 years, this was the only practicable solution.

The most controversial feature of Spanish rule in the Americas was the treatment of the indigenous peoples. Whilst the conquest of the New World was an undoubted disaster for its inhabitants (the population of Mexico dropped from an estimated 25 million in 1500 to around 1 million by 1600), much of the 'Black Legend' of Spanish atrocities in the Indies is based on propaganda and special pleading. In this, the fiercely humanitarian writings of Bartolomé de las Casas proved influential, although he would never have intended that his writings be used to discredit Spain. One example of the need for correction to the traditional picture is the relationship between the Church and the native peoples. The missionary orders made energetic efforts at education, alms provision and evangelisation, working tirelessly to improve their conditions of life. Moreover, contrary to contemporary Protestant propaganda, they sought to incorporate the Indians' culture into worship. The extent of the state's efforts can be gauged by missionaries' investigations into pre-colonial religion in the Americas, the publication of grammars for the indigenous peoples' languages and the great survey of colonial life undertaken by Philip's Finance Minister, Juan de Ovando, in the 1570s. This culminated in the promulgation of the Ovando Code, a codification of law and customs for the Americas, which established that the Indian population of the Americas had certain inalienable rights, which the settlers could not abrogate. Whilst this did not guarantee fair treatment for the surviving Amerindian population, it did provide a framework within which the state could, when it had the time and energy to do so, bring the more brutal of the settlers to book.

3 The State of the Empire in 1556

> **KEY ISSUES** How healthy, economically and politically, was the Spanish Empire at the time of Philip's accession? What structural problems did Philip encounter in ruling the Spanish Empire?

Philip II's inheritance was a difficult one. Although the mightiest empire on Earth, Spain's greatness was feared and resented by its neighbours, and the extent of its possessions made it vulnerable at numerous points. Charles I's long wars with France and the Ottomans had strained its finances and military and economic resources to breaking point. Philip was faced with a dangerous conjuncture of problems. Although he has been criticised for the ineffectiveness of his response to the challenges facing him in 1556, some of the difficulties he faced were impossible to resolve.

Of all the problems inherent in ruling such a vast empire, transport, communications and the defence of outlying provinces were the most impossible to overcome. Communications from Mexico took at least four months to arrive in Madrid, those from Peru at least nine months, and those from the Philippines could take two years! Within Europe, correspondence could travel remarkably quickly, especially when the news carried was vitally important, but adverse weather or other difficult circumstances could cause dreadful delays. Messengers were occasionally intercepted, robbed or even murdered, and Catalonian bandits even raided convoys carrying gold to Barcelona for shipment to Italy. Such complications meant that the time taken for a letter to travel from Brussels could vary from nine days to 90, and this unpredictability was highly disruptive to effective government. In February 1575 Don Luis de Requesens, Philip's governor in the Netherlands, wrote to his brother, Don Diego de Zuniga, in Paris:

> I do not know how your Lordship fares for letters from Spain; for myself, I have heard nothing from the King concerning the affairs of the Netherlands since 20th November last ... His Majesty's service has suffered greatly by it.[8]

Consequently subordinates could avoid implementing unpopular decisions or delay passing on unpalatable news to the King. Braudel concludes that:

> 1 The enormous Spanish Empire ... depended upon what was for the period an unprecedented combination of land and sea transport. It required not only continual troop movements but the daily dispatch of hundreds of orders and reports ... The Spanish Empire, which was

5 poorly situated from the point of view of its European and world possessions, expended the better part of its energy in struggles against distance.[9]

Philip's problems were exacerbated by the fact that he inherited
an empire at war with France, threatened by the Turks in the
Mediterranean and the raids of the Moslem pirates, and facing
serious financial and economic problems. Despite substantial annual
imports of gold and silver bullion from the Indies, the empire was
bankrupt in 1556. His income, roughly 3 million ducats in 1556, was
dwarfed by a national debt of 25.5 million ducats, and servicing this
debt absorbed roughly half of Spain's annual revenues. There was
little chance that Philip could increase taxes to balance his budget,
since, as the Venetian ambassador observed in 1559, 'His Majesty's
revenues are very limited, because he cannot add to them by imposing taxes except with the consent of all his people'.[10] Furthermore,
the economic growth that had sustained Castile for the previous
century was gradually grinding to a halt and the *Cortes* was already
protesting that their towns could not continue paying taxes to sustain
the King's wars. In 1557, Philip was forced to declare bankruptcy.

Amidst these immense problems, the King had somehow to try to
maintain his inheritance. In his struggles to do so, he relied heavily
upon the contributions of his 'foreign' possessions, especially in the
military sphere. Castile's *tercios* marched alongside German and
Italian mercenaries, armed with Milanese artillery and paid for with
loans from Genoa and Portugal and with silver from the Indies.
Philip's navy was, in 1556, predominantly Italian, commanded by the
Genoese admiral Doria, and the Armada fleet of 1588 contained a
large Portuguese contingent, as well as German and Ragusan ships.
His most successful general in the Netherlands was an Italian,
Alexander Farnese, Duke of Parma. This illustrates the extent to
which the *monarquia* did function as a single entity, but it also reveals
the degree to which Spain was incapable of bearing the burden of
empire unaided.

Consequently, although this era is often referred to as the 'Golden
Age' of Spain, Kamen suggests that Spain never really possessed the
economic and financial strength necessary to support an empire the
size of Philip's inheritance, and that the seeds of Spain's later decline
had been sown by Charles I:

> By imposing upon Spain the Burgundian territories and other obli-
> gations, Charles forced it to take on the leadership of an empire which
> neither its military nor its economic capacity had earned.[11]

References

1 Cited in H. Kamen, *Philip of Spain* (Yale, 1997), p. 29.
2 Cited in *Ibid.*, p. xi.

3 Venetian Ambassador Badoero, cited *Ibid,* p. 210.
4 P. Pierson, *Philip II* (London, 1975), p. 40.
5 Cited in G. Parker, *The Grand Strategy of Philip II* (Yale, 1998), p. 42.
6 Cited in Pierson, *Philip II,* p. 43.
7 Cited in *Ibid.,* p. 45.
8 Cited in F. Braudel, *The Mediterranean in the Reign of Philip II* (Collins, 1973), p. 356.
9 *Ibid.,* pp. 371-2.
10 Ambassador Suriano to the Senate of the Venetian Republic, 1559, cited in J. C. Davis, *The Pursuit of Power* (Harper, New York, 1970), p. 42.
11 H. Kamen, *Spain: 1469–1714: A Society in Conflict* (Longman, 1991), pp. 161–2.

Summary Diagram
Philip II's Inheritance

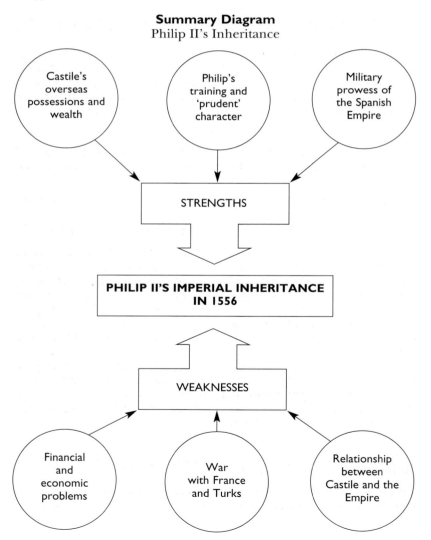

Working on Chapter 2

This chapter has mainly examined Philip's inheritance. Organise your notes around the three sections of the chapter. Use the section headings as your sub-headings and copy down the Key Question(s) for the section underneath each heading. Then, in your own words, write down the key points you would use to answer the question, including relevant factual detail to back up your points. Sometimes it is helpful to use colour for your main points or to indent the factual detail, to help separate it from the general points.

Answering structured questions on Chapter 2

Whilst it is unlikely that you would be asked to write an essay on Spain at the outset of Philip's reign, the issues addressed in this chapter might form a part of a structured question. Structured questions tend to focus on a particular aspect of a topic and require a concise and focused response. They usually take one of the following forms:

Describe; What; How; Explain; Why.

These sorts of question demand that you demonstrate good factual knowledge and an ability to list a number of relevant factors. The question below is typical:

1. **a)** Describe the relationship between Spain and her colonies in the Indies.
   b) How strong and prosperous was Spain at the accession of Philip II?

Part b) of this question requires that you demonstrate knowledge and understanding of the state of Spain in 1556. Since the question focuses particularly on Spain, you should not spend too long on the rest of the empire in your answer. The question divides into two issues, 'strong' and 'prosperous'. To assess how 'strong' Spain was in 1556, you should consider her international position, as well as the size and strength of the empire. Sources of weakness included the dispersed and disconnected geographical nature of the empire, the difficulties of communications and the regionalism of the provinces, especially Aragon. Her economic and financial health is the main consideration when evaluating Spain's prosperity in 1556. In this question, balance is an important quality in a good answer. The examiner would expect you to deal more or less equally with 'strong' and 'prosperous'.

Source-based questions on Chapter 2

Sometimes you will be given sources to use as stimulus material for a broader discussion of an issue. In such questions, you will often be invited to use your own knowledge alongside the extracts. The question below is typical of this kind of task.

1. The 'Problems of Empire' in 1556

Study the map of the Spanish Empire in Europe on page 15, and read the extracts from Braudel on pages 18–19 and Kamen on page 19.

a) Read the extract from Kamen on page 19. What were Philip's 'Burgundian territories' (line 1)? *(2 marks)*

b) Using the map on page 15, explain why communications with Philip's possessions in the Netherlands were so difficult. *(4 marks)*

c) What problems did Philip face at the time of his accession to the throne of Spain? *(6 marks)*

d) To what extent were the difficulties Philip faced in governing the Spanish empire made worse by his character? *(8 marks)*

3 Philippine Government and Administration

POINTS TO CONSIDER

This chapter examines Philip II's government of Spain and her empire. Philip's approach to government has often been criticised as slow-moving, hamstrung by a lack of trust and an obsessive desire to control personally even the tiniest details, although his defenders point out that Philip's extensive and effective intelligence system made him the best-informed ruler in Europe, although this necessarily generated bureaucracy. His defenders cite Philip's use of formal and informal *juntas* (governing committees) to formulate policy, as well as the conciliar system that he inherited from his father, as evidence of a more delegatory style of government. This debate leads us into a consideration of the nature of the 'Prudent King'. Construct simple diagrams showing the structure of the government at various points of the reign so as to better appreciate the relationship between various structures and individuals within the regime.

KEY DATES

1566 Death of Gonzalo Perez, Philip's State Secretary. Philip appoints, as his replacements, his son, Antonio Perez, and Gabriel de Zayas.
1577 Murder of Juan Escobedo, on the orders of Antonio Perez.
1579 Perez arrested. Cardinal Granvelle hereafter chairs the Council of State and the *Junta Grande*.

1 Philip's Approach to Government

> **KEY ISSUE** To what extent was Philip a 'Paper King'?

Philip possessed a strong sense of his personal responsibility for the empire and its people. Consequently he chose to govern as a personal ruler. The problem with such an approach was that he possessed a world empire, which generated a tremendous quantity of work. Around the King a huge bureaucracy grew up, consisting of court officials, councillors and ministers, drawn from the aristocracy and from the growing ranks of *letrados* (university educated, legally trained civil servants).

Philip's government became a by-word for slow-moving, bureaucratic and hesitant decision-making, and historians and contemporaries have placed much of the blame for this squarely on Philip himself. He refused to allow any one individual to possess all the reins of government or even to have access to all the relevant knowledge on a given issue, insisting that all government business, important or not, pass across his desk in the form of '*consultas*' prepared by the secretaries of the various councils. His personal secretary from 1573, Mateo Vazquez, described this method of working.

1 Papers were dealt with in this way. His Majesty used to sit down at his table and the secretary came up to it with his papers. Sitting on a stool, Vazquez would make a report to His Majesty on what those secret letters and memorials on serious matters contained. When His Majesty
5 had listened, he decided what he wished to be done in each case ... The secretary at once took a note of His Majesty's resolutions and subsequently turned these into memorandums for the ministers concerned in the King's name ... If the matter was serious the memorandum was written by Vazquez, but initialled by the King ... When His Majesty
10 dealt with *consultas* secretary Vazquez would read out the substance of them with the Council's recommendation and His Majesty having heard their contents, took the decision which seemed the best in each case in the presence of the secretary. The latter noted down a decision on a sheet of paper and afterward, using the most clear and concise reasons,
15 he put the decision in the margin of the *consulta* in handwriting, which the King subsequently initialled.[1]

Philip demanded accurate and regularly updated information and so he established a huge imperial archive at Simanças. Every regional governor was ordered to produce 'full reports of all his provinces, cities, towns, sites, wildernesses, rivers, of their advantages civil and military, their finances, manufactures and tributes ...'.[2] This data gave Philip an impressive overarching grasp of his realms.

Extracts from a Questionnaire on the Spanish American Empire (1577–1586).

1 The Governors ... shall ... distribute this printed Instruction and Memorandum throughout their jurisdiction to all towns of Spaniards and Indians.
QUESTION 3. State in general the climate and quality of the said
5 province or district; whether it is cold or hot, dry or damp, with much rainfall or little and at what season there is more or less ...
QUESTION 14. State to whom the Indians belonged in heathen times and what dominion was exercised over them by their lords; what tribute they paid and the form of worship, rites and customs they had, good
10 or bad.
QUESTION 22. Describe the native trees that commonly grow wild in said district; and what benefits to be gained from them, their fruits and their wood ...
QUESTION 23. Mention whether the cultivated trees and fruit trees in
15 the district brought there from Spain or elsewhere grow well or not.
QUESTION 28. Describe the gold and silver mines, and other veins of metal or minerals, and mineral dyes there may be in the district ...

QUESTION 33. Describe the trade and commerce and dealings by which the Spanish and native inhabitants of the town support them-
20 selves ...

QUESTION 35. Note the cathedral or parish churches in each town, with the number of benefices and prebends in each; if the town contains any chapel or noteworthy endowment, state what it is, and who was its founder.[3]

Philip possessed the finest ambassadorial network and courier system in Europe. This meant that he often knew more of events in other European states than their own ambassadors, but although he was probably better informed than anyone else in Europe, his government did not function any better for it. This was because, once he had gathered all the relevant documentation on a given subject, he routinely consulted with several different advisors or councils before issuing his final decision. Recognising that this approach was inefficient Philip appointed Cardinal Espinosa in 1566 to supervise his business. However, this experiment foundered when Philip grew frustrated with Espinosa's preference for transacting business verbally without committing matters to paper so that Philip could oversee his work. After Espinosa was shunted off to semi-retirement in 1572, Philip took direct control of government again. Thereafter, he relied upon the two State Secretaries and his personal secretary, Mateo Vazquez, but none of these were permitted to control all aspects of the King's business.

Unfortunately, whilst his desire to keep abreast of important matters is understandable, Philip's advisors frequently complained that he was unable to distinguish between the important and the trivial. In 1589, Juan de Silva bemoaned 'the attention that His Majesty pays to details of little consequence ... It is lamentable that he wastes time in these things ... His Majesty's head is capable of absorbing a vast quantity of business but does not distinguish between what he should reserve for himself and what he should entrust to others.'[4] Philip's secretaries were called to working lunches, he read dispatches in his carriage while travelling, and he worked long, exhausting hours at his desk, often far into the night, considering carefully every document and all manner of requests. Despite this, perhaps because of it, he was often overwhelmed by the sheer volume of governmental business and government ground to a halt under an avalanche of paper. The Venetian Ambassador described him at work.

1 I am reliably informed by someone who frequents his private apartments that he is never idle, for besides his desire to read himself all the incoming and outgoing correspondence of all areas, and from all the ambassadors and ministers of his vast dominions ... he writes
5 every day with his own hand more than a ream of letters, between *billetes*, *consultas* and orders, which he constantly sends to his councillors, judges, secretaries and ministers in this way, and countless other

> secret business that he handles with other individuals. It is hardly to be
> believed how much time he spends in signing letters, licences, patents
> 10 and other affairs of grace and justice: on some days it amounts to
> 2,000 [items/documents].[5]

During May 1571, a busy period, with preparation for the imminent
campaign against the Turks and the ongoing crisis in Granada occupying the King's attention, 1252 papers passed across the royal desk.
Meanwhile, in the Netherlands, Alva anxiously awaited replies to his
own reports, but was told by a contact at court: 'It is the same thing
that your Excellency knows and has experienced – papers and more
papers, and more of them every day'.

Philip was occasionally so overwhelmed with work that he neglected important matters. During the 1566 uprising in the
Netherlands, Philip's advisors most experienced in Dutch affairs
urged him to visit the province and resolve the crisis personally.
However, assailed by contradictory views from other ministers, and
uncertain of the best course of action, Philip hesitated for months
before dispatching Alva with an army to pacify the rebellious
provinces ahead of a royal visit. However, by the time Alva reached
the region, the vice-regent Margaret of Parma had calmed the situation, so Alva's subsequent repression was counter-productive.
Philip's frequent changes of mind between 1565 and 1567 succeeded
in creating an impression of double-dealing and insincerity that
deeply damaged his affairs in the Netherlands. Gonzalo Perez, writing
in 1566, reflected on Philip's handling of Dutch affairs.

> 1 His Majesty loses track of things, and will continue to do so, by treat-
> ing them with different persons, this time with one, this time with
> another, and hiding them from one, and revealing them to another; and
> thus it is not surprising that different orders go out, even contradictory
> 5 orders.[6]

Philip's frustrated ministers and secretaries pleaded with him to prioritise and delegate more, expressing concern that he was becoming
a 'paper King', distant and inaccessible, and so obsessed with trivial
matters that he was neglecting his kingdom and people. But Philip
was temperamentally incapable of doing so, and the consequences
were often disastrous.

Philip's desire to 'micromanage' affairs, denying his local representatives and military commanders the freedom of action they
required to respond to changing events, and sending frequent dispatches with orders and suggested courses of action, proved calami-
tous on occasion. During the Armada campaign, Philip was still
sending Medina Sidonia orders for the invasion of England in
September 1588, unaware that the remnants of the battered and
broken fleet were only a few days from docking at Santander, having
already been defeated. Even at the end of his reign, his correspon-

dence with Diego de Chaves Orellana, *corregidor* (governor) of the *Cuatro Villas* (four strategically important ports on Spain's northern coast), demonstrates his desire to know everything and control everything, no matter how trivial. On 15 May 1595, the King ordered the movement of a group of disabled galley slaves to Santander.

> 1 Diego de Chaves Orellana, *corregidor* of the *Cuatro Villas* ... The five
> criminals sentenced to the galleys, of whom you write in your previous
> letter, whom you have imprisoned in Laredo as unfit for service, are to
> be sent to Santander, into the charge of Fernando de la Rivaherrera,
> 5 who has been instructed to admit them and restore them to health ...[7]

A year later, he wrote to Chaves Orellana giving an account of a recent military action within the governor's own area of responsibility! The King's desire to make the most trivial decisions left the governor with little to do but obey.

All of this meant that the government of Spain slowed to the pace at which the King could process the documentation that passed across his desk. As the popular witticism in the colonies had it; 'If death came from Spain, we would all live to a ripe old age'.

2 The Role of Castile in the Empire

> **KEY ISSUE** What was the relationship between the Castile and the 'provinces'?

One criticism of Philip's government was its Spanish, indeed Castilian, bias, and this too stemmed directly from the King himself. Philip was born in Castile, brought up in Castile and spoke (fluently) only Castilian. Spaniards dominated his court and councils and he leaned heavily upon Spain for money and fighting men. The position of Castile within the empire was, consequently, a sensitive issue. Philip's decision in 1561 to reside in Madrid and rarely to visit his other dominions possessed a certain organisational logic, but the centralisation of government alienated his more distant subjects, who did not dispute Philip's right to rule, but did question the apparent subjection of the rest of the empire to Castile. One Aragonese nobleman complained 'They [Castilians] give the impression that they alone are descended from heaven, and the rest of mankind are mud'. Outside Spain, Philip's tendency to appoint Spaniards to important posts (most of his governors in the Netherlands, from Alva onwards, were Spanish) alienated the local elites. Things were not helped by the attitude of Spaniards towards the rest of the empire. One Castilian official commented 'These Italians, although they are not Indians, have to be treated as such'.

However, Philip II cannot be accused of being unfamiliar with his possessions beyond Castile. He was the most extensively travelled ruler of the age. Between 1548 and 1551, he conducted a grand tour of his father's empire, from Aragon to the Netherlands, via Italy. He resided for long periods in Brussels and, during an exhausting 'road trip', visited and was sworn in as heir in every one of the 17 Dutch provinces. During 1554-6, he spent a difficult two years in England. He remained in Flanders, co-ordinating the war against France until his return to Spain as King in 1559. Despite allegedly concluding 'It is neither useful nor decent to travel around one's dominions', Philip visited Aragon again in 1591 and after the acquisition of Portugal in 1580 he ruled the empire from Lisbon for the next three years. He even made plans to travel to the Netherlands in 1567, but was persuaded to wait until Alva had pacified the province.

Moreover, Philip's decision to govern from Madrid was a logical response to the problem of ruling so gigantic an empire. A permanent bureaucracy was required for this task, and the logistics favoured the establishment of a fixed governmental centre. As Gonzalo Perez observed in 1564, 'Since Spain is the principal member from which we must cure and restore all the others, I do not know how His Majesty could leave it'.[8] Other contemporary rulers were arriving at the same conclusions. The growth of early modern government demanded the evolution of more complex and substantial governmental structures, and Philip's decision simply reflects his awareness of the impossibility of continuing in the peripatetic tradition of late-medieval kingship (wherein the King was always on the move and had no fixed capital).

Nonetheless, it remains true that Philip had a preference for Spaniards around him, and that his perspective on the world became increasingly short-sighted as he grew older. Although we can point to the handful of non-Castilian ministers (Ruy Gomes da Silva, Cardinal Granvelle, Idiaquez and Moura), the Castilian aristocracy dominated the Court. The Venetian ambassador noted in 1559 that:

1   The King ... has no esteem for any nation except the Spanish. He consorts only with Spaniards, and with these only he takes counsel and governs. Moreover, contrary to the custom of the Emperor, he takes no notice of Italians and Flemings, and least of all Germans, and although
5   he retains the chief men of each nation in his kingdom, still it is observed that he declines to admit any one of them to his secret councils.

3 The Conciliar System

> **KEY ISSUE** What was the conciliar system and how effectively did it function?

Philip presided over the largest administrative apparatus in early modern Europe, and despite efforts to make it more efficient it

became ever more complex and many-headed as the reign progressed. The heart of the system was a series of councils, created by
his father in the 1520s, which monitored specific areas of policy.
Philip's experienced Secretary of State, Gonzalo Perez co-ordinated
these and acted as an intermediary between King and councils,
especially the Council of State, which the State Secretary usually
chaired. The Council of State (or Council of Castile) was theoretically
the most senior of the bodies advising the King, since it encompassed,
as well as many of Philip's ministers, the heads of the greatest noble
families. However, in practice, the Council of State exercised less
influence than it might have, due to Philip's preference for using
specialist councils for specific areas. The Councils of Aragon, Italy,
Portugal (after 1583) and the Netherlands (after 1588) administered
these particular geographical areas. The Council of Castile did oversee a number of specialised bodies, including the Councils of Finance
and War, which dealt with these two crucial issues for the whole
empire, and the Council of the Indies, which dealt with all colonial
business. Separate from the other bodies, and responsible to Philip
alone, was the Council of the Inquisition (which in Spain was a government, rather than a church, institution), responsible for implementing religious policy within the peninsula.

This network of bodies formed the sphere in which the real business of government was done, but their over-lapping memberships
and areas of authority provided frequent opportunities for factional

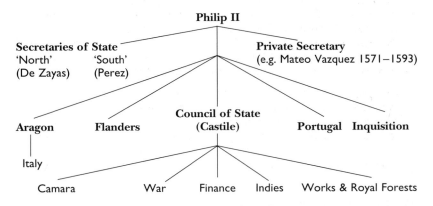

The Conciliar System. Inherited from his father, the system of councils that
administered the empire was altered only marginally during Philip's reign.
The councils of Portugal (1583) and Flanders (1588) were added to help
govern these difficult possessions, although it is remarkable how long it
took the King to establish a body to coordinate policy for the Netherlands.
Access to the King was also via his state and private secretaries, who
consequently became powerful individuals.

rivalries at Court to spill over into government business. For example, the Council of State's duties included overseeing Spain's diplomatic and military interests within Europe, including the military in the Netherlands and Italy, despite the existence of the two provincial councils and the Council of War. Conflict between the committees was exacerbated by Philip's tendency to consult individually with representatives of each body on matters that crossed departmental boundaries.

The conciliar structure of Philippine government generally worked well and ensured that, whilst the empire was theoretically federal, it was, at the same time, centralised. Crucially, it offered the only possible means whereby the King could manage his immense administrative load. Hence Philip instructed government servants throughout the empire to deal with the appropriate body, rather than address their correspondence to him personally. In the event, of course, neither his ministers nor the King observed these instructions to the letter, and on controversial matters, especially during the era of the Alva-Eboli factional conflicts (see below), the King was often swamped by personally addressed memoranda and demands for time-consuming audiences (which he disliked and discouraged). Philip tried to keep abreast of all business by receiving daily '*consultas*' from each council, wherein the conciliar secretaries summarised the day's business for him, even on occasion drafting letters and orders and presenting them to the King simply requiring his signature. Even so, the volume of business grew so rapidly that, by the 1590s, the key councils met practically on a daily basis.

On occasion, the King short-circuited the conciliar system by forming one-off '*juntas*' (executive or advisory committees) to deal with specific issues. The Council of Flanders evolved out of an informal junta that sat increasingly often to deal with the affairs of the Netherlands, and one-off committees dealt with preparations for the Lepanto and the Armada campaigns.

Inevitably there were numerous occasions when two or more councils took an interest in a single issue, and there were frequent struggles between committees for control of policy in a given case. Often Philip left his ministers and advisors to fight it out, but his preference for consulting several different groups meant that he often received different (and competing) advice. This fuelled factional conflict.

4 The Secretaries of State, Factional Conflict and the Perez Affair

KEY ISSUES How far did factional conflict at Philip's Court affect the conduct of government? What were the consequences of the 'Perez Affair'?

In such a system, the State Secretary came to possess tremendous influence, given that he saw the king on a daily basis. At the outset of his reign, Philip's old servant Gonzalo Perez, occupied this role, and he held the balance between the feuding factions of the Court in the early years of Philip's reign. After Gonzalo Perez's death in 1566 Philip split the role between two men, Perez's son, Antonio, who took overall responsibility for the peninsula, Italy and the Indies, and Gabriel de Zayas, who took responsibility for the Netherlands and Franche Comte.

Although Philip was theoretically a personal monarch, possessing enormous authority over the whole of Spanish life, from economic regulation to war and peace to religion, his 'absolute authority' was effectively restrained by the workings of court faction, an ever-present feature of early modern government, both in Spain and elsewhere. Factional conflict amongst Philip's advisers was an inevitable problem, given Philip's preference for keeping a range of opinions around him at Court whilst trusting none of his ministers with complete knowledge of policy. From the outset he was served by two principal groups, the Toledo grouping, headed by the hawkish Duke of Alva, and the Eboli faction, led by the King's friend and confidant, Ruy Gomes da Silva, Prince of Eboli. These factional groups dominated the Council of State and the conciliar structure and drew into their ranks the State Secretaries, de Zayas being cultivated by Alva, and Antonio Perez belonging to the Eboli circle, more or less inheriting its leadership after Eboli's death in 1572. During the first decade of the reign Ruy Gomes da Silva, a consummate courtier, was pre-eminent, probably because of his close personal friendship with the King and because 'he attended upon him without harassing him or obstructing him when he desired solitude ... He performed his duties ... with eager willingness and to the liking of his lord'.[9] By contrast, his rival, the Duke of Alva's more robust, soldierly attitude in the king's presence damaged his position at Court during this period.

The importance of this factional rivalry has been much debated. Philip evidently encouraged the rivalry of the two principal factional groupings, so as to defuse their potential to control policy, but historians differ over the consequences of this. The 'positive' view argues that factional interest groups and powerful, ambitious individuals sought to control the patronage system and to influence policy, and that their rivalry provided the Crown with a dynamic means of channelling talent and energy in its service. The 'negative' view argues that Philip's active promotion of factional conflict at Court was damaging, and that these aristocratic cliques expended such energy in a constant struggle for primacy at Court that the business of the state suffered.

The 'Perez Affair' is perhaps the most famous example of the problems created by Philip's encouragement of competing factions at Court. In 1577, Philip dispatched his half-brother, Don Juan, to the Netherlands, with orders to regain control of the rebellious provinces. Not entirely trusting Don Juan, Philip, probably on the advice of his secretary of state, Antonio Perez, dispatched a young aide, Escobedo, to keep tabs on the situation. However, Escobedo became an ally of Don Juan, and when he returned in 1578, he came as his representative to Philip, to deny allegations that Don Juan was scheming to put himself on the throne of England as Mary Stuart's husband. His arrival panicked Antonio Perez, by then the effective leader of the Eboli faction, who seems to have been behind these suggestions. Fearing the revelation of his role in blackening Don Juan's name and misleading Philip regarding the situation in the Netherlands, Perez convinced the King that Escobedo was a traitor and, apparently on his own authority, had the young man murdered. Philip's own role in the Escobedo's murder remains shrouded in mystery. Perez subsequently gave several different versions of events, exonerating Philip under torture in 1590, but later, after his escape from custody and flight to Aragon, changing his story, to suggest that Philip ordered the crime. Marañon, Perez's biographer and probably the best authority on the affair, concludes that Philip was a party to the plan, since he seems to have obtained the approval of his confessor, Chaves, beforehand. Marañon does, however, suggest that Perez duped Philip into approving this course of action.

Whatever the tortuous facts of the case, Philip must have known Perez to be responsible, but allowed the act to go unpunished. However, almost from the moment of Escobedo's death rumours abounded that Perez was responsible, and gradually Philip began to have doubts about the State Secretary's reliability and honesty. At this point, Perez's many enemies struck. Indeed, Perez's fall probably owed as much to his arrogance and the workings of court faction as it did to Philip's conscience. In 1579, Mateo Vazquez presented the King with a dossier of evidence on Perez's corruption, alleging his involvement in the Princess of Eboli's attempts to obtain for her son the Portuguese throne, which Philip regarded as rightfully his. Philip secretly recalled Granvelle, then serving as his ambassador in Rome, and on the very day of Granvelle's arrival, Philip had Perez and La Eboli arrested on corruption charges. A long game of cat and mouse ensued, since Perez had hidden away as a sort of insurance policy numerous documents relating to the Escobedo affair. Repeatedly imprisoned and then released over the next decade, Perez eventually, under torture, admitted to having had Escobedo murdered, but after his escape and flight to Aragon in 1590 he repudiated his confession and implicated Philip in the affair. Arrested again by the Inquisition, on a trumped-up charge of heresy, he was released by a mob, and in the ensuing chaos of the Aragonese Revolt, escaped to exile in France. He spent the rest of his life in London and Paris, writing highly damaging propaganda against Philip II. His *Defence Memorial*, and his highly selective use of often-distorted documents to attack Philip during his English and French exile damaged Philip's reputation and contributed to the 'Black Legend'.

5 Later Expedients: The Junta Grande and the Junta da Noche

KEY ISSUE How did Philip change his approach to government in the later stages of his reign?

After 1580, Philip changed his approach to government. The conciliar system remained the basis of the administrative system, but Philip increasingly governed through a series of informal committees, which revolved around a tight-knit group of key figures at court. This was, in part, a reaction to the Perez Affair, which damaged Philip's faith in his previous approach of balancing the court factions. Philip used the opportunity of Perez's arrest in 1579 to free himself from the competing Eboli and Alva factions. Instead he formed a 'second ministry' around Granvelle, Don Juan de Idiaquez, Don Juan de Zuniga and Don Cristobal de Moura. (Interestingly, considering the frequent accusation that the King was too Castilian in his outlook, Granvelle was Burgundian, Idiaquez a Basque, Zuniga Catalonian and Moura Portuguese.) The change in approach may also have reflected a belated recognition on Philip's part that the business of government was growing too immense to be carried out effectively by the King alone. This committee, which had no formal constitutional existence, but operated informally, half within the Council of State and half outside it, was nicknamed the *Junta Grande*, and it became the heart of the regime for the remainder of Philip's life. Gradually an inner committee evolved, comprised of Moura, Idiaquez, the King's Secretary Mateo Vazquez and a floating additional membership according to need. This was nicknamed the *Junta da Noche* (Committee of the Night), because it gathered in the King's chambers after the work of the day had been completed to review major issues of the day and formulate policy. The *Junta da Noche's* domination of royal policy was resented by the Castilian grandees in the Council of State, where Alva's heir, Don Hernando de Toledo, led the opposition.

Even in the last few years of Philip's life he was still trying to pull all the strings at the heart of the governmental system, but illness and tiredness meant that he was forced increasingly to delegate the day-to-day business of government to the *Junta da Noche* and his son Philip. Even so, the King was still actively engaged in the business of government.

6 Analysis: How Absolute was Philip II?

KEY ISSUE Was Philip an 'absolute monarch', in theory or in practice?

A central pillar of the 'Black Legend' has been the argument that

Philip ruled Spain and his empire as an absolute ruler, above the law. Although this can be supported by a number of arguments, there are weaknesses in virtually every strand of this case. Whilst Philip's official pronouncements often claimed that he governed by 'divine right', deriving his power and authority from God, there is little real evidence that he actually exercised power in an absolute manner.

Critics have argued that his desire to control every aspect of the bureaucracy and government of the Empire from his palace in Madrid reflected an absolute temperament and a desire to rule as a divine right monarch. There is an element of truth here. Philip attempted to rationalise the laws and customs of his realm in order to make his regime more effective. However, although his achievements in codifying the laws of Spain, Portugal, the Americas and the Netherlands were impressive, this process was fraught with dangers. The attempt to simplify the laws and customs of the Netherlands in the hope of forging them into a single province, governable from Spain, contributed to the outbreak of revolt in the region (see pages 45–7), since the local nobility feared that this would mean the imposition of Spanish ways. However, whilst Philip clearly sought to control the tiniest details of the administration, we must nonetheless make a distinction between appearance and reality – Philip's efforts to exercise comprehensive day-to-day control over affairs across the empire were self-defeating. Bogged-down in detail and paper, he often failed to see the 'big picture', and this prevented him from exercising a truly absolute authority.

Equally, whilst it has been suggested that the Cortes of Castile and Aragon declined as a check to royal power during Philip's reign, this seems to be contradicted by the furore over taxation that erupted in the 1591 Cortes of Castile (see page 41). Philip was forced to negotiate with the Cortes of Aragon over taxation, even after 1591 and the defeat of the Aragonese Rebellion (see pages 43–5). Indeed, despite his desperate financial straits, Philip never introduced arbitrary taxation within Spain, always being careful to seek the support of the political nation for changes in the *alcabala*, or for the imposition of new taxes. Even the *millones* (see page 81) was only levied after the approval of the Castilian Cortes.

On the other hand it is clear that the Crown possessed extensive powers over two important areas of the state, the military and the Church. Philip's absolute authority over military matters enabled him to respond uncompromisingly when faced with rebellion in Granada (1568–1570), the Netherlands (1566–1609) and Aragon (1590–1). Likewise, in practical terms he was as powerful over the Spanish church as his contemporary Elizabeth I was over the Church of England. Indeed, Lynch has described Philip's powers over the church as 'probably more complete in Spain in the sixteenth century than in any other part of Europe'.[10] Both of these areas provided the Crown with immense stores of patronage with which to purchase the support and co-operation of the Spanish nobility.

There were moments when Philip acted in a 'tyrannous' fashion, perhaps most famously in his judicial executions of the Dutch grandees, Hornes, Egmont and Montigny. However, even at these times, he took care to have his actions legitimised by a panel of Spanish judges, and he always cited 'reasons of state', although this hardly excuses his ruthless treatment of his enemies. In general, however, he seems to have had a strong sense of his duty to uphold justice and very rarely interfered in the courts.

The conciliar system of government meant that the power of the Crown was mediated through a series of lesser authorities, central government councils, viceroys and governors, and informal juntas. Even so, ultimate authority derived from the Crown and the holders of posts at any level of the government system could be, and were, replaced at the whim of the King. Thus, Parma was recalled from the Netherlands in 1592 and Medina Sidonia felt unable to resist his appointment as the commander of the Armada in 1588, even though he regarded himself as quite unsuited to the role, and desperately wished not to take it on.

More meaningful a restriction on royal authority was the constant state of factional warfare amongst ministers and magnates at Court, which Philip seems rather misguidedly to have fostered. Equally, poor communications and inefficiency, an inevitable by-product of the size of the *monarquia*, made delegation and decentralisation of day-to-day decision-making inevitable. This was particularly so in the New World, where the viceroy necessarily exercised considerable independence of judgement.

Although some historians have suggested that Philip II, in his preference for *letrados* (university-trained lawyers and bureaucrats), reduced the power and status of the great nobles during his reign, the evidence simply does not support this conclusion. If anything, the aristocracy expanded its powers during Philip's reign. The financial difficulties of the monarchy meant that Philip progressively auctioned off the crown's estates and *senorios* (areas of Royal jurisdiction) to overcome temporary cash flow problems. These were almost invariably bought by ambitious magnates like Medina Sidonia and Mendoza, who assembled huge *latifundia* (estates on which the nobility possessed actual judicial power) and private armies numbering several thousand men.

The best indication of the limitations of Philip's royal authority is the success with which the Aragonese nobility resisted what they perceived as encroachments upon their regional *fueros*. Similarly the longevity of the Dutch Revolt suggests that royal power was not absolute. As the reign progressed, the growth of contractual theories of government in Spain suggests that Philip's subjects did not regard him as absolute, although they may have feared that he wished to become so. Juan de Mariana, the Jesuit political theorist, wrote that 'the King must be subject to the laws laid down by the state, whose authority is greater than that of the king'.[11] If even the theoretical basis of royal absolutism was beginning to come under attack, then it seems clear that the argument that Spain was an absolute monarchy is flawed. Most modern historians have concluded we should judge the Spanish state not by its theoretical absolutism but by the practice of government. Any attempt to do this leads us inescapably to the conclusion that Philip's Spain was not an absolute monarchy.

References

1 Cited in Jones, *Europe 1450–1650* (Nelson, 1997) p. 291.
2 Baltasar Porreño, *Dichose ychechos del rey D. Felipe II* (1628, Madrid 1942), pp. 6–7.
3 Taken from O'Day et al. ed, *Culture & Belief* (Blackwell, 1990), pp. 343–351.
4 Cited in H. Kamen, *Philip of Spain* (Yale, 1998), p. 278.
5 Cited in J. C. Davis, *The Pursuit of Power* (Harper, New York, 1970), pp. 85–6.
6 In G. Parker, *Guide to the Archives* (Brussels, 1971), p. 27.
7 Letter of Philip II to Diego de Chaves Orellana, 15 May 1595. See http://www.lib.byu.edu/~rdh/phil2.
8 Cited in Parker, *The Grand Strategy of Philip II*, p. 91.
9 Cabrera de Cordoba 'Felipe II' (Vol II) p. 140–141, cited in J. M. Boyden, *The Courtier and the King* (Berkeley, 1975), p. 123.
10 J. Lynch, 'Philip II and the Papacy' in *Transactions of the Royal Historical Society* (1961) p. 24.
11 Cited in H. Kamen, *Spain 1469–1714: A Society of Conflict* (Longman, 1983), p. 150.

Summary Diagram
Spanish government

Philip II And Spanish Government

Pressures	Solutions	
• Far-flung Empire	• Permanent capital at Madrid	
• Immense administrative burden	• Conciliar structure of government	
• Factional conflict at Court • The Perez Affair	• Juntas	• Junta Grande • Junta de Noche • 'One-off' Juntas
• Philip's personal managerial weaknesses	• Secretaries of State	
• The place of Castile in the Empire	• Personal government by the King – effective?	
How effective was Philip's government of Spain?		
How 'absolute' was Philip II?		

Working on Chapter 3

You will need to have good notes on the workings of Philippine government, as an understanding of the systems of government and their limitations is essential to any attempt to explain the success and failure of Philip's reign as a whole. Write out the key questions and subquestions for the chapter and make concise bullet point notes on each. Make sure that these bullet points include essential factual information and evidence to support the points you have made. Write a brief concluding paragraph answering the key question at the end of each section of your notes.

As suggested in the Points to Consider section at the start of this chapter, a diagram or table containing a 'snapshot' of the governmental structures at the outset of the reign, in the 1570s and towards the end of the reign, would be useful too, as this would show how Philip adapted his approach to government over the course of his reign.

The central issue to grasp in this chapter is the inter-relationship between Philip's character and the complex systems of imperial government. When you have completed your note-making, write out a brief, note-form summary of this issue.

Answering structured questions on Chapter 3

Most examinations now contain structured questions, and these require that you demonstrate accurate and concise factual knowledge. Factual knowledge will not be sufficient on its own to gain you a good mark, however. You will need to exhibit an ability to explain and account for events, and in particular to assess the causes and consequences of events.

I **a)** Why was the role of Castile in the Philip II's *monarquia* resented by the rest of the empire?
   b) What were the effects on Philip's government of his practice of encouraging factional rivalries in his councils?

Part a) of this question requires an evaluative answer. Questions beginning with 'Why' demand the consideration of a range of factors. For example, in this question some of the following points might be offered: Philip II rarely visited other parts of the empire, preferring to govern from his palaces around Madrid; Philip II surrounded himself with Castilian ministers; Castilians were appointed to important posts in the other provinces; other provinces resented the perceived arrogance of Castilians towards them, and the assumption that Castile was the heart of the empire. Try to evaluate the relative importance of the points that you have made and consider the consequences for Philip's imperial government of the hostility between the provinces of the empire. Finish your answer with a conclusion. A well-argued and consistent conclusion is an essential component of any high level answer, and you should ensure that yours answers the question clearly and precisely and gives your opinion (although it is considered stylistically clumsy to write 'I think' or 'in my opinion' in an essay, so don't do this).

Part b) of this question appears to be merely descriptive, but you should not simply describe the two factions at Court and their conflicts. Try to assess the effects of these conflicts on the conduct of government. Central to your answer will be the consequences of the Perez Affair, which resulted in the fall of Philip's talented, but overambitious, State Secretary. The ripples of this affair spread into other areas of policy, affecting the situation in Aragon, for example. Remember that historical events are connected to one another in all sorts of ways, and that cause and effect interconnect across the artificial boundaries of topics that historians create so as to organise their work. Thus, the factional conflict and the Perez Affair relate to internal government, the 1590-1 uprising in Aragon, the ongoing revolt of the Netherlands and Philip's reputation abroad. Be prepared to make these sorts of connections in your answers, even if this means thinking outside the boundaries of this chapter.

Source-based questions on Chapter 3

1. Philip II's Style of Government

Study the memoir by Mateo Vazquez on page 24, the extract from the Questionnaire to Spanish America on pages 24–5 and the letter by the Venetian Ambassador on pages 25–6.

a) What do these extracts from the Questionnaire to Spanish America reveal about the Spanish government's interest in the colonies? *(4 marks)*

b) How far do the descriptions of Philip at work by Mateo Vazquez and the Venetian ambassador support one another? *(4 marks)*

c) How valuable a source of information for the historian investigating Philip II's government is the letter by the Venetian ambassador? *(4 marks)*

d) Using these sources and your own knowledge, consider the argument that Philip II governed the empire ineffectively because he was a 'Paper King'. *(8 marks)*

4 Opposition and Revolt

POINTS TO CONSIDER

Philip II's rule was challenged by revolts in Granada, Naples, Aragon and the Netherlands, and the cumulative effect of these rebellions was disastrous for Spain. Why was Philip II's authority challenged in so many corners of his empire? How effectively did he deal with these protests? What were the consequences for the empire of these challenges?

KEY DATES

1566	Iconoclastic rioting in the Netherlands.
1567	Philip dispatches Alva to the Netherlands with 20,000 troops.
1568	William of Orange's attempted uprising fails.
	Moriscos Revolt in Granada initiates two years of civil war.
1572	Second Dutch Revolt breaks out.
1576	'Spanish Fury' at Antwerp results in the Pacification of Ghent.
1579	Union of Arras returns the southern Dutch provinces to the Spanish fold, but the Union of Utrecht cements the alliance of the northern, rebel provinces.
1581	Act of Abjuration. 'United Provinces' depose Philip as their sovereign ruler.
1584	Assassination of William of Orange.
1585	English join the Dutch revolt, in the Treaty of Nonsuch.
	Riots in Naples are crushed.
1590–1	Aragonese Rebellion.
1596	Philip grants the southern Dutch provinces to the 'archdukes' Albert and Isabella.

Philip II faced challenges to his authority from various parts of his *monarquia*. This opposition took a variety of forms. Although Castile was the foundation of Philip's power, the Castilian Cortes nonetheless frequently challenged his demands for taxation and, as the reign progressed, his imperial policies. Elsewhere, opposition often took a more serious form. Rioting and protests against taxation disrupted government in most corners of the empire, including the Indies, and in Spain itself, the Moriscos Revolt in 1568 and the Aragonese Revolt of 1590-1 shook the King's authority. However, the most serious and debilitating challenge to Philip's rule took place in the Netherlands, where rebellion dragged the Spanish into a bitter and prolonged conflict that resulted in defeat and financial ruin.

1 The Cortes

KEY ISSUE How far, and how effectively, did the Cortes seek to restrain Philip's power?

Whilst the Castilian Cortes historically had little right to challenge the Royal will it would be false to regard it as powerless and irrelevant during Philip's reign. The Cortes served three main functions. It confirmed royal legislation and presented grievances or offered advice to the King, but its main function was to vote occasional subsidies (*servicios*) and to approve changes in the rate of the *alcabala* and *encabazemiento*. This gave it significant leverage over the Crown, especially one so strapped for cash as Philip's. A bitter argument disfigured the Cortes of 1566-7, when the deputies refused to grant the *servicio* until grievances had been addressed. Philip resisted these protests successfully, but his failure to address grievances stored up opposition for the future. He increased the *encabazemiento* in the 1570s, but was forced after another fractious Cortes in 1576–7 to reduce the tax again. In 1591, the deputies of the Cortes, summoned to approve the extension of the *millones*, expressed their growing impatience with the King's constant wars and demonstrated that they were no Royal poodles. Pedro Tello, a former soldier, requested that:

1 With your great prudence and that of your highest councils you suspend these wars for now as best you can, while maintaining in the Atlantic a large navy capable of protecting your fleets to and from the Indies and around your coasts, for God knows that in the attempt (to
5 defeat your enemies) Your Majesty has spent his last strength and is under no obligation to do more.[1]

Although they did approve the extension of the tax, the Cortes outlined a contractual theory of taxation when they argued that, if the terms of the grant were not met, then 'the Kingdom will have no obligation to continue with it'.[2]

As the reign progressed, the Castilian Cortes met more frequently and for longer periods. This counsels us against accepting too readily the view that they became subservient to Philip's will. Their ability to approve or obstruct the collection of taxation made them essential allies of the Crown. Philip had to control and cultivate them. Bullying did not work, and by and large, Philip did not resort to such tactics.

2 The Moriscos' Revolt

KEY ISSUE Why, and with what consequences, did the Moriscos of Granada rebel against Philip's rule in 1568?

The reconquest of Spain from the moors (North African Moslems) at the end of the fifteenth century left a substantial population of converted Moslems (*Moriscos*) in Spain, especially in the kingdom of Valencia, where one in three people were Moriscos, and in the province of Granada, where Moriscos comprised 54 per cent of the 'population. Although a succession of edicts and missionary efforts secured their outward conversion to Catholicism by 1526, the Moriscos never genuinely converted, and the efforts of the Inquisition to enforce their nominal Christianity were piecemeal and ineffective, baulked by stubborn resistance from both the Moriscos and their Christian landlords, who protected their labour force from the Inquisitors' 'troublemaking'. Moriscos continued secretly to practise their former faith, wore their traditional clothes and, in the more remote areas, retained their language and customs. Consequently, many Spaniards regarded the Moriscos' loyalty as suspect, and prospective Christian settlers cast covetous eyes over their land. Nonetheless, the Moriscos remained peaceable and never troubled the Spanish government, despite persistent rumours that they were in league with the Barbary pirates who raided the Spanish coast so freely.

During the 1560s, Philip's government stepped up the pressure on the Moriscos, increasing the taxes on leather and silk, their principal industries. Furthermore, the use of *'convivencias'* (arrangements whereby, in return for a fine paid to the Inquisition, Morisco communities were left alone) was abruptly ended by Inquisitor-General Valdes, who stepped up attempts to eradicate Morisco customs and culture, which the government regarded as evidence of their continued attachment to Islam. The failure of the 1567 harvest increased further the desperation of the Morisco population and, on Christmas Eve, 1568, the Moriscos of Granada, 30,000 mostly unemployed silk-weavers, rose in revolt.

Although the uprising became largely confined to the Alpujarras hills, where the entire population rose up, the government feared that it might spread to Valencia and Aragon, and that it might attract Turkish support. Consequently Philip dispatched a military expedition, headed at first by the local magnate, the Marquis of Mondéjar, whose initial success in recapturing more than 180 villages nonetheless could not bring a swift end to the rebellion. In 1569 he was replaced by the King's half-brother, Don Juan, commanding 20,000 hastily raised Spanish troops. The revolt dragged on for two more years and has been described as 'the most savage war to be fought in Europe that century'.[3] Both sides committed massacres, fuelled by religious and racial hatred. At Galera, 2,500 Moriscos, men, women and children, were slaughtered by Spanish troops. By 1570, the rebels had been forced into the most inaccessible and inhospitable corners of the Alpujarras mountains, and when the authorities offered a free pardon to all those willing to surrender, the final resistance crumbled. With the surrender of the rebel leader, Aben Humeya, the revolt ended.

With the suppression of the revolt, the government decided in 1571 to distribute the Granadan Moriscos across the peninsula, with predictably tragic human consequences. Perhaps 120,000 Moriscos died during their forced resettlement, from disease, famine and mistreatment. Furthermore, they were exposed to renewed persecution from the Inquisition in the 1570s, with some areas (e.g. Valencia) witnessing a thirty-fold increase in prosecutions, although executions were rare. The economy of Granada was seriously disrupted. Despite the dispatch of 50,000 Spanish settlers to the region, the population of Granada fell by 28 per cent and its towns, whose population fell by 33 per cent, experienced a catastrophic decline. Inevitably, industrial and agrarian activity fell too. The state could take little pleasure in the outcome of the war. The campaign cost 60,000 Spanish lives and 3 million ducats over two years, and the brutally ineffective efforts to restore order demonstrated the weakness of the Spanish state. The Moriscan problem remained unresolved until the reign of Philip III.

3 The 'Liberties' of the Provinces – The Aragonese Revolt

> **KEY ISSUE** How effectively did Philip govern the kingdom of Aragon?

As we have seen, Philip II inherited a complex patchwork of peoples, customs, laws, and 'liberties' that did not, logically, belong together. The provincial elites regarded themselves as equal partners with their Castilian counterparts in a dynastic '*monarquia*', and frequently emphasised that, never having been conquered, they owed loyalty to Philip, not Castile. Gregorio Lopez Madera observed, in 1597:

> All past monarchies were created by violence and force of arms. Only that of Spain has had just beginnings, a great part having come through successions, and the rest through conquests based on just titles.[4]

Given the provinces' proud assertion of their liberties, any failure by Philip to consider on an equal status with Castile the needs of his other possessions almost invariably resulted in unrest. Following poor harvests and a rise in the price of bread, the city of Naples rose in revolt in 1585. The measures taken by the viceroy to restore order (31 'rebels' were executed, 71 sent to the galleys and 300 exiled) typified Philip's hard-line towards rebellion but did little to regain the trust of his Neapolitan subjects. For the most part, however, Philip's Italian possessions accepted the rule of his chosen viceroy. Philip ran into much more intractable problems when governing Aragon.

The Aragonese nobility were a thorn in Philip's side from the outset of the reign. The extent of Aragon's autonomy can be gauged from a report written by the Venetian ambassador Suriano in 1559.

1　The Aragonese claim to be independent and to govern themselves as a
　republic of which the king is head. He may not succeed to the govern-
　ment unless they have elected him. They are so zealous to preserve
　their independence that they contest every little thing to prevent the
5　king from having greater authority over them. They make difficulties
　even where they have no right, so that Queen Isabella used to say that
　her husband, King Ferdinand, would have been pleased if the crown of
　Aragon had actually rebelled, since then he would have been able to
　reconquer it and impose his own laws.[5]

In the first year of Philip's reign, 1556, the execution of some bandits
by the viceroy of Aragon, Francavila, resulted in rioting in Zaragoza in
defence of Aragon's *fueros* (provincial liberties), although the protest
also gave voice to a feeling of abandonment by the King which had its
origins in Charles I's long absences from the peninsula. Philip visited
Aragon on his way home from the Netherlands in 1559 and was sworn
in as monarch, and thereafter he managed Aragon cautiously, asking
the kingdom for little taxation and rarely summoning the *Cortes*. He
took great care throughout his reign not to breach Aragon's '*fueros*'.
However, on the other hand, he visited Aragon infrequently, and not
at all between 1563 and 1585, and the local nobility felt increasingly
ignored by their sovereign. This neglect may have contributed to the
lawlessness of the kingdom, and Philip became increasingly frustrated
by the endemic banditry and unrest between Christians and Moriscos
in the county of Ribagorza, which resulted in massacres of Morisco villages in 1585 and 1588. This situation was complicated by the personal rivalry between the local magnate, the Duke of Villahermosa,
and Philip's minister, the Count of Chinchon. In an attempt to
restore order Philip forced Villahermosa, who was accused of encouraging the lawlessness, to sell the county to the Crown in 1588.

　In the same year, Philip appointed a Castilian, the Duke of
Almenara, as his viceroy, with the intention of cracking down on the
kingdom's endemic lawlessness. Although the appointment of a
Castilian to govern Aragon was quite legal, it was volubly resisted by
the local nobility and was unquestionably a provocative act. Soon
afterwards, by chance, Antonio Perez escaped from custody in Madrid
and fled to Aragon, claiming the right of a native of that kingdom to
be tried in the *Justiciar's* court. Philip was not prepared to stand by
whilst Perez was tried by his fellow Aragonese, in open court, where
he could make allegations about Philip's involvement in the
Escobedo murder (see page 32), and so he ordered the Inquisition,
which had jurisdiction over religious offences in Aragon, to arrest
Perez on heresy charges. However, the attempt to arrest Perez in May
1591 resulted in rioting and Almenara was killed by the mob. A
second outbreak of rioting in September resulted in a noble revolt in
Zaragoza, which drew in (reluctantly, it would appear) the young
Justiciar, Jean de Lanuza. Although the countryside around the city

remained calm, Philip could not afford to allow such rebellion to go unanswered, especially given his experience in the Netherlands, and for once he acted decisively. An army of 14,000 troops moved rapidly to Zaragoza, preceded by reassuring propaganda stressing Philip's commitment to Aragon's *fueros*, and within four days of their arrival, the troops had restored order. Lanuza and 22 other prominent rebels were executed and Perez fled to France, where he continued to publish his allegations about Philip's conduct of government, which fuelled the 'Black Legend' with French and English audiences.

With the rebellion suppressed, Philip personally attended the Aragonese Cortes of 1592, reaffirming the *fueros* of Aragon and its constituent kingdoms. However, he also reiterated his right to appoint the viceroy, instituted majority voting in the Cortes and excluded the younger nobles from its meetings. These measures ensured more orderly government in the kingdom and strengthened royal authority, whilst preserving Aragons's autonomy. Such cautious and balanced handling of local liberties and fears contrasted strongly with Philip's handling of the Netherlands, and shows that the King was capable of learning from his mistakes.

4 The Revolt of the Netherlands

> **KEY ISSUES** Why did Philip's Dutch subjects rebel in the 1560s and 1570s? Why did Spain fail to suppress the Dutch Revolt?

Perhaps the greatest disaster of Philip's reign was his failure to subdue the Netherlands Revolt, which began in 1566 and rumbled on into the seventeenth century. The revolt became a millstone around the neck of the *monarquia*, and Philip's treatment of the rebels earned him widespread criticism throughout contemporary Europe. Even the Castilian Cortes criticised his handling of the conflict, and the Jesuit, Juan de Palafox, concluded that 'nobody doubts that the wars in Flanders have been the ruin of this monarchy'.

a) The Origins of the Revolt

The Netherlands were the wealthiest part of Philip's empire, highly urbanised, with a relatively advanced economy based upon commerce and the production of woollen cloth. Antwerp was the economic centre of Northern Europe, although already, even before the revolt, Antwerp's dominance of Northern European commerce was ending.

The Netherlands had been united with the Habsburg monarchy by Philip's father, Charles I. Charles, who was born in Flanders, enjoyed good relations with his Dutch subjects, and handled the Dutch carefully, understanding and respecting their jealous protection of their 'liberties'. Ruling the Netherlands was a delicate business. Philip II was Duke, Count, Governor or Stadtholder in each province individually. When absent he governed through a regent, traditionally advised by the greatest Dutch nobles. Philip's first regent was his Aunt, Margaret of Parma, who headed a 'national' government in Brussels. The central legislative body was the States-General, composed of representatives from each of the provincial States. The States General delivered grievances to the ruler, but could only approve taxes after consulting representative bodies in each province, town or district. Consequently decision-making was painfully slow and a myriad of local rights and privileges had to be taken into consideration. Charles had generally treated these bodies with great care, dropping legislation that met with opposition and shelving taxes if

The Revolt of the Netherlands, 1566–1609.

any protest was registered, but Philip quickly lost patience with this, seeing it (largely correctly) as a means through which to evade the collection of taxation.

The Dutch uprising in the 1560s was partially caused by religious problems. Officially Roman Catholic, the Netherlands contained numerous Protestants, despite the execution of 2000 Protestant heretics during Charles' reign. After 1556, the growth of Calvinism in the Netherlands threatened a fresh wave of heresy and Philip undertook to crush this menace, despite the reluctance of Dutch magistrates to convict their neighbours on heresy charges.

Philip II didn't handle the Netherlands as skilfully as Charles had. He spoke no Dutch, and his court in Brussels was Spanish in character. He thus quickly created an impression of caring little either for the region's provincial privileges or for the political interests of the local elites. After his return to Spain in 1559, the distance between the King and his Dutch subjects made them difficult to rule and reinforced their impression that Philip cared little for his Dutch subjects. This may have been unfair on Philip, who professed in 1560 to be missing the Netherlands, and who made plans in 1567 to visit the provinces, before circumstances forced him to abandon them.

Philip's problems in the Netherlands began in 1559. The reopening of the border between the Netherlands and France following the treaty of Câteau-Cambrésis allowed French Calvinists to enter the Netherlands, especially after the outbreak of the religious wars in France. Philip wanted to establish Spanish military garrisons along the French border, but the States-General opposed the proposal, which was criticised as expensive. This was the first of many clashes between Philip's regency government in Brussels and the leading noblemen of the region, nicknamed the 'Grandees'. Margaret of Parma found these powerful figures difficult to manage, and their resentment of the influence possessed by her chief advisor, Cardinal Granvelle, complicated matters further. Philip's 1561 plan to revitalise the Church in the Netherlands by increasing the number of bishoprics in the region engendered further conflict. The nobility resented the creation of several new bishoprics outside of their gift and churchmen were unhappy that these new creations were to be financed out of their existing incomes. Virtually everyone in the region feared that this would pave the way for the introduction of the Inquisition, which would threaten the relative tolerance of heresy that many Netherlanders saw as crucial to their commercial success. In 1563, the Grandees forced Philip to scrap the plan and reassign Granvelle away from the Netherlands, but the issue poisoned relations between Philip and the Dutch nobility.

Things did not improve with Granvelle's removal. During 1564 and 1565, a trade depression and a fierce winter saw unemployed weavers rioting for food. In order to reduce tension, Margaret loosened the Heresy Laws, sending the Count of Egmont to Spain to explain why.

He returned with a letter suggesting that Philip had offered a (rather vague) compromise on religion, but a second letter confirmed that Philip remained uncompromising regarding heresy. The resultant confusion over Philip's intentions only undermined the position of Margaret of Parma and created a political vacuum in which a political difficulty became a full-blown crisis.

In April 1566, a group of dissenting Dutch nobles known as the 'confederates' forced Margaret to accept the 'Compromise of the Nobility' cancelling the Heresy Laws. This, in turn sparked-off a sudden upsurge of Calvinist preaching and outbreaks of iconoclasm (the destruction of church buildings and decorations by bands of Calvinist rioters). Margaret sent urgently to Philip for support and, after a long debate in his Council of State between the moderates led by the Prince of Eboli and the hard-liners led by the Duke of Alva, Philip dispatched an army, commanded by Alva, to pacify the province. However, the army took months to assemble and during this time the Dutch Grandees, alarmed by the rioting, assisted Margaret in restoring order. Unfortunately this came too late to prevent the arrival of Alva in August 1567 with 10,000 crack troops. On his arrival Alva immediately took charge, as Philip had instructed him. He arrested a number of prominent Dutch nobles and established a court, the 'Council of Troubles', to prosecute those responsible for the 'revolt', prompting Margaret to resign and William of Orange, the most senior Dutch nobleman, to flee to Germany. This was a prudent move on William's part. Alva executed the Counts of Hornes and Egmont in 1568 and in Spain, Margaret's latest envoy, Montigny, was secretly garrotted on Philip's orders. William of Orange's lands and titles were confiscated and his eldest son was arrested and taken to Spain as a hostage. This prompted an attempted rising, led by Orange, which failed miserably. During the next few years, the 'Council of Troubles' arrested more than 12,000 people for their part in the disturbances, executing more than 1,000.

b) The Second Revolt

Having pacified the provinces, Alva initiated a series of reform projects, codifying Dutch law, reforming the universities and introducing Philip's much-delayed 'bishoprics plan'. However, Alva's regime was very unpopular, and his attempt to modernise the tax system by introducing a series of new taxes, the Hundredth Penny (a one-off 'poll tax') and the Twentieth and Tenth Pennies (sales taxes not unlike Spain's *alcabala*) was deeply resented, coinciding as they did with another trade depression and a harsh winter, which caused widespread suffering in 1571.

Consequently, the people of the Netherlands were thoroughly dissatisfied with Alva's government when William of Orange, with help from German and French Protestants, launched a five-pronged assault on the Netherlands in the spring of 1572. Alva's veteran troops repulsed the invasions from Germany and France with ease, but the rebels in the North, spearheaded by a group of Calvinist pirates known as the 'Sea Beggars', entrenched themselves in several fortified towns, forcing Alva to embark on a series of long and difficult sieges during 1572 and 1573. Here, Alva miscalculated, adopting a brutal policy of slaughter towards any town that forced him to besiege it. Mechelen, Naarden, Zutphen and Haarlem all witnessed appalling massacres which, although successful in cowing the resistance of neighbouring towns, only reinforced the determination of William of Orange's ardently Calvinist rebels, holed-up in Holland and Zeeland. After the Haarlem massacre Granvelle, by now Philip's ambassador in Rome, wrote to the King, questioning Alva's policy. 'The Duke of Alva now complains that the other areas have not surrendered spontaneously, but he should remember that there are soldiers defending the towns who, fearing the same treatment as the garrison of Haarlem, will fight on until they die of hunger.'[6] Although eventually Philip replaced Alva with a new governor, Requesens, and a policy of moderation, the damage had been done. Spain became embroiled in a desperate, drawn-out struggle, which consumed ever-greater resources and which contributed to the state declaration of bankruptcy in 1575.

FERNANDO ALVAREZ DE TOLEDO, THIRD DUKE OF ALVA (1507–1582)

-*Profile*-

The Duke of Alva, Spain's greatest nobleman and the leader of the Toledo faction at Philip II's court, was 'the greatest soldier of his generation',[7] but his reputation is forever tarnished by his brutal treatment of surrendered towns during the Dutch Revolt.

His military reputation was forged in Charles V's German wars and in the Italian campaign against France and the Papacy in 1557. A trusted advisor of Philip II, he helped negotiate the Treaty of Câteau-Cambrésis in 1559 but fell out of favour at Court during the 1560s, where the King preferred the counsels of his rival, Ruy Gomes da Silva, Prince of Eboli. Alva advocated a strong, uncompromising line against the Dutch in 1566, and subsequently he was dispatched to restore order in the province in 1567. He crushed Orange's uprising in 1568, and established a largely successful regime in the Netherlands, despite being starved of funds from Spain. He wisely counselled Philip against intervening in support of Catholic rebels against Elizabeth I of England during 1570–1. However, his policies in the Netherlands resulted in

Detail of Peter Breughel's 'Massacre of the Innocents', showing Alva as Herod.

revolt in 1572, and the extreme measures he adopted to restore order resulted in his recall to Spain, where Alva retired to his estates in 1574. Recalled in 1580 to command the invasion of Portugal, his outstanding success in this campaign revived his fortunes, but he died in 1582, before he was able to enjoy his restoration to the centre stage in Spanish political life.

Although remembered primarily for his bloody suppression of the Dutch, Alva's career amounted to much more than this one appalling episode, which perhaps illustrated his tendency to seek a soldier's solution to political problems when under stress. The unsophisticated butcher of Haarlem was in fact a skilful and under-rated politician.

Source 1. Maltby assesses Alva's Qualities.

1   As a statesman ... he was above the common run ... He saw the purposes of foreign policy with crystal clarity, but was at the same time wordly enough to be flexible about the means. If at times he overreacted ... he was normally patient and cautious ... His master
5   might send out fleets and armies with a pious 'God will provide' but Alva had seen fiascos and catastrophes beyond Philip's home-bred imagination and was disinclined to leave things to chance.[8]

Source 2. Peter Breughel the Younger's portrayal of Alva as Herod in his 'Massacre of the Innocents': see page 50.

Source 3. Alva, to Philip II, in 1573, on the Eve of the Siege of Alkmaar.

1   'I cannot refrain from beseeching Your Majesty ... to disabuse yourself of the notion that anything will ever be accomplished in these provinces by the use of clemency. Things have now reached the stage where many Netherlanders who until now have been
5   begging for clemency now see and admit their mistake. They are of the opinion that not a living soul should be left in Alkmaar'.[9]

Source 4. Maltby Summarises Different Views of Alva.

1   Alva is remembered not because he was a great soldier and statesman but because he is a symbol. To [Spain] ... he is the epitome of virtue; devout, spartan, courageous, prudent and above all loyal ... to his church and king ... To much of the rest of the world
5   he is ... the epitome of intolerance, cruelty and harsh fanaticism.[10]

Questions

1. Using Sources 1 and 4, summarise Maltby's view of Alva's strengths and weaknesses. *(3 marks)*
2. How useful would Breughel's painting be to the historian assessing the career of Alva in the Netherlands? *(5 marks)*
3. How far does Alva's letter (Source 3) support Maltby's assessment of Alva (Source 4)? *(4 marks)*
4. Using all the sources and your own knowledge, explain why Alva's policies in the Netherlands were so counter-productive. *(8 marks)*

By 1576 the Spanish position in the Netherlands had broken down completely. Requesens died early in the year and, inconceivably, Philip dithered over the appointment of his replacement, finally sending his headstrong half-brother, Don Juan, in 1577. During this interregnum, the Spanish army fell apart, mutineers storming Antwerp, looting the town indiscriminately and killing thousands. This 'Spanish Fury' led the Dutch provinces to sign the Pacification of Ghent, by which they agreed to work together to expel the Spanish troops and establish an autonomous government. Unable to resist, Philip instructed his representatives to accept the terms offered, but the truce lasted only as long as Spain's financial weakness.

c) The 'Dutch Ulcer'

In 1578, a bumper yield from the Indies treasure fleet and the signing of a truce with the Turks changed the situation. Philip dispatched fresh troops under Alexander Farnese, Duke of Parma, and the campaign against the rebels was renewed, together with a diplomatic offensive which exploited emerging gaps between the radical Calvinists in the northern provinces and the Catholic southern 'loyalist' provinces. During the next decade, Parma scored a series of victories over the rebels, recapturing large areas of the country. The assassination of William of Orange in 1584, an act rewarded by Philip II, seemed to signal the beginning of the end for the rebels. Antwerp fell shortly afterwards and despite the intervention of English troops in 1585, victory seemed within reach. Why, then, did Spain fail to retake the Netherlands? Quite simply, Philip took his eye off the ball at the crucial moment. From 1587 onwards, Philip constantly diverted Parma's forces from their Dutch campaigns. In 1588, Parma was ordered to join up with the Armada for the invasion of England. In 1590 and 1592, Parma marched (reluctantly) to the aid of French Catholics fighting the Protestant King Henry IV. Each time Spanish forces withdrew from the provinces, their enemies utilised the breathing space to resupply, reorganise and fortify their positions. In 1591, Maurice of Nassau even launched a counter-attack, recapturing Breda and setting back the Spanish cause in the Netherlands several years. Moreover, the prioritisation of conflicts with England and France (see page 54) diverted finances and resources away from the Netherlands. Starved of funds, the Army of Flanders resorted once more to mutiny. In frustration, Parma refused to march into France in 1592, which resulted in his removal as commander in the Netherlands.

During the 1590s, the front-line stabilised. Even Philip's appointment of the moderate Archduke Albert and Philip's daughter Isabella as joint rulers of an autonomous (self-governing) Netherlands could not save Spanish rule in the North, which had by now declared itself an independent state – the 'United Provinces'. The conflict dragged on for a further decade after Philip's death in 1598, but the outcome was never really in any doubt. A truce was signed in 1609, which effectively recognised the independence of the northern provinces.

d) Philip II and the Dutch Revolt

The rebellion of the northern provinces of the Netherlands against Spanish control succeeded for a number of reasons. The dogged determination of William of Orange and his supporters, especially the Calvinist minority, who knew that there would be no mercy for them under a restored Spanish regime, provided an uncompromising nucleus for the rebel cause. The Calvinists asserted their control over the northern provinces to such an extent that, when the United Provinces of the Netherlands finally declared formal independence from Spain, the official religion was Calvinism. There were other factors in the Dutch victory. The geography of the region favoured the rebels. The Netherlands, once described by an English visitor as the 'great bog of Europe', was criss-crossed with wide rivers. Large areas were reclaimed land, below sea level and protected by dykes, which the rebels destroyed, flooding the countryside so as to force the Spaniards to raise the siege of Leyden in 1573. The military geography was equally favourable to the uprising. Several of the rebel-held towns possessed modern fortifications that enabled them to hold out for months against Spain's forces. The Dutch made effective use of these advantages, rarely venturing out to engage the superior Spanish forces in an open battle and strengthening the existing fortifications at every opportunity. After the death of William of Orange in 1584, his younger son Maurice of Nassau took over the military command of the rebels and proved to be an inspired and innovative general, who forged the armies of the rebel provinces into an effective fighting force, capable of taking the offensive for the first time.

Even so, Philip II bears the greatest responsibility for the loss of the northern provinces. His attempt to impose policies that, although seeming eminently sensible in Spain, breached the traditional 'liberties' of the Netherlands laid the foundations of the division between himself and his Dutch subjects. When decisive action might have prevented trouble in the 1560s, he dithered. His replacement of the moderate Margaret of Parma with the warlike Duke of Alva restored order but by methods that alienated many hitherto neutral Dutch citizens. The behaviour of Spanish forces, both under Alva's command during 1572–3 and when in mutiny after 1575, can be laid partially at the King's door, if only because his denial of adequate resources to the Army of Flanders increased the likelihood of mutiny. His rigid adherence to an intolerant religious policy was entirely justifiable within a sixteenth century context. He argued that 'If . . . other sovereigns do not allow their subjects to have a religion other than the one they themselves profess, for reasons of state as well as religious motives, why then should this attitude be denied to me'.[11] But whilst this approach is understandable, his inflexibility and inability to compromise at crucial moments, and his willingness to offer concessions only when bankrupt and in possession of what his enemies knew was a weak hand, meant that he missed opportunities to resolve the revolt peacefully. Finally, his involvement of the Spanish empire in conflicts with France and England in the 1580s and 1590s led to the adoption of a defensive posture in the Netherlands at precisely the moment when Parma had victory in his sights, and thereby let the hard-pressed rebels off the hook. Moreover, the inevitable bankruptcy that resulted in 1596 from this over-commitment finally deprived his forces everywhere of the funds necessary to win. Notwithstanding the brilliant political manoeuvring of William of Orange, and the outstanding military leadership of his son, Maurice of Nassau, the survival and ultimate victory of the Northern rebels was more the result of Spanish (i.e. Philip's) failings than the inspired efforts of the rebels.

References

1 Cited in J. Lynch, *Spain 1516–1598* (Blackwell, 1991), p. 485.
2 Cortes of 1596, cited in G. Woodward, *Philip II* (Longman, 1992), p. 20.
3 H. Kamen, *The Spanish Inquisition* (Phoenix, London, 1997), p. 224.
4 Cited in H. Kamen, 'Early Modern Spain: The Difficulties of Empire' in *History Sixth* 2, pp. 2–6.
5 Suriano, cited in J.C. Davis, *The Pursuit of Power* (Harper, New York, 1970), pp. 41–2.
6 Cited in G. Parker, *The Dutch Revolt* (Pelican, 1977), p. 160.
7 W. Maltby, *Alba* (Berkeley, 1983), p. 306.
8 *Ibid.*, p. 307.
9 Cited in Parker, *The Dutch Revolt*, p. 161.
10 *Ibid.*, p. 307–8.
11 Philip II to the King of Denmark, 1586. Cited in J. Lynch, 'Philip II and the Papacy', in *Transaction of the Royal Historical Society* (1961), p. 34.

Summary Diagram
Opposition And Revolt

How much opposition did Philip II face across the Empire 1556–98?		
Constitutional opposition by representative Institutions	**Open Revolt**	**Discontent and rioting endemic to Early Modern state**
• Castilian Cortes • Aragonese Cortes • Dutch 'States-General'	• Moriscos' Revolt in Granada, 1568–1570 • Dutch Revolts 1566–68 1572–76 1577–1609 • Aragonese Rebellion 1590–1591	• Indies • Protests against the *Millones* • Naples, 1585

Why was Philip faced with such opposition?				
Regional 'Liberties'	Financial/ Tax Demands	Economic Crises	Religious Policy	Philip's mishandling of situations

Working on Chapter 4

This chapter has addressed some of Philip II's greatest challenges. Organise your notes around the four sections, using the diagram above or the section headings as your overview headings. Note that a lot more space has been given to Philip's handling of the Dutch Revolt. This reflects the seriousness of the revolt for Spain. For many historians, the failure to deal effectively with the rebellion in the Netherlands was the most significant failure of Philip's reign, and consequently good notes are needed. The complexity of the conflict means that a timeline of key events is a good place to start. You then need to identify turning points in the conflict, as well as ensuring that your notes cover the Key Issues identified in this chapter. It is likely that a little wider reading would help you to grasp the centrality of this issue for Philip's reign (see Further Reading at the end of this book).

Answering structured and essay questions on Chapter 4

The opposition Philip experienced often features in both structured questions and essays. In order to answer structured questions effectively, you need to have a good factual knowledge of the key events, but questions will require that you use this information to put forward a clear view about why and with what consequences a given event occurred. Look at the following two questions.

I. **a)** Why did the Moriscos of Granada rebel against Philip's government in 1568?
 b) What does Philip's response to the uprisings in Granada (1568–1571) and Aragon (1590–1) reveal about his handling of opposition?
2. **a)** Explain why Philip II's policies aroused opposition in the Spanish Netherlands in the 1560s.
 b) How effectively did Alva restore royal authority in the Netherlands between 1567–1572?

In Question 1, part a) demands that you demonstrate knowledge and understanding of historical causation. This questions invites you to assemble a differentiated list of factors. Try to organise these around themes (for example, religious issues, economic issues, the effectiveness of Philip's government) and try to prioritise between the reasons you offer for the revolt. Make sure that you finish your answer with a well-argued and consistent conclusion that answers the question clearly and precisely.

Part b) of this question requires a more evaluative answer, which compares Philip's handling of two serious challenges to his authority. What are the similarities and differences between the State's response to rebellion in Granada and Aragon? Was the different nature of the revolts (the Moriscos were protesting essentially about religion, whilst Aragon was defending its *fueros*) significant? Did Philip appear to have learned anything from his earlier experiences with rebels by the time Aragon rebelled in 1590?

Essay questions on this chapter will mostly concern the Dutch Revolt.

I. Consider the arguments for and against the claim that Philip II was largely to blame for causing the Revolt of the Netherlands.
2. How important was religion in the revolt of the Netherlands?
3. Why, despite her military superiority, did Spain fail to suppress the Dutch Revolt?

As the questions above indicate, questions on the Dutch Revolt tend to focus on the origins of the conflict or on the reasons for the Spanish defeat. Question 3 above is a fairly straightforward example of a 'Why?' question. The most effective way to approach such a question is to compile a list of statements beginning with the phrase; Spain failed to suppress the Dutch rebels militarily because . . .

a) the geography of the Netherlands favoured the rebels

b) the rebel cause was led effectively by William of Orange and his son Maurice of Nassau

c) Spain failed to finance their armies in the Netherlands consistently

d) Philip and his governors in the Netherlands frequently mishandled the Dutch politically.

Try to make a list of 5 or 6 factors and then prioritise among them. Make sure that each point you make is thoroughly supported with evidence and ensure that your answer contains a concluding paragraph in which you summarise your arguments and answer the question.

5 Religion: Establishing Orthodoxy

POINTS TO CONSIDER.

Critics of Philip II's highly controversial religious policies portray him as a fanatic, bent on exterminating, with the assistance of the Spanish Inquisition, those who did not share his faith. Although modern historians have substantially revised this view, stressing the reforming efforts of both the state and the Holy Office, nonetheless it is on questions of religion that the Black Legend has been most enduring. As you read this chapter, reflect upon this image. Is it merited? Consider a) how far the Spanish church was reformed and improved during Philip II's reign, and b) to what extent, and by what means, Philip sought (and achieved) a uniformly orthodox Catholic Spain.

KEY DATES

1557 Inquisition arrests Archbishop Carranza of Toledo. A protracted diplomatic battle with the Papacy follows.
1558 Lutheran cells discovered at Valladolid and Seville.
1559 Autos da Fé at Seville and Valladolid result in the burning of 77 Lutherans.
1564 July. Philip II promulgates the Decrees of the Council of Trent in Spain.
1566 Carranza case referred to Rome.
1568 Moriscos of Granada rise in revolt.

Philip II was a devout and loyal Catholic, and his religious policy was absolutely uncompromising. He famously told Pope Pius V that, 'rather than suffer the least damage to religion and the service of God, I would lose all my states and a hundred lives if I had them; for I do not propose or desire to be the ruler of heretics'.[1] We should, however, be cautious in taking this as an absolute statement of policy. He was almost certainly trying to convince the Pope of the wisdom of dispatching the Duke of Alva and 10,000 Spanish troops to the Netherlands. Nonetheless, it was a matter of principle for Philip II that his realms should be maintained free of heresy, either Protestant or Islamic. However, he also attempted to improve the quality of the Spanish Church. The decrees of the Council of Trent were enforced enthusiastically in Spain, and a series of active, energetic bishops were appointed. The Holy Office of the Inquisition was employed, not simply in persecuting heretics, but also in monitoring and reporting on the progress of the reform programme. Finally, Philip actively promoted the interests of Catholicism beyond Spain's borders. He took an interest in the ministry to the indigenous peoples of Spain's American and Far Eastern possessions and he attempted, with unfortunate results, to reform the Church in the Netherlands. Geoffrey Parker has argued that Philip's sense of religious mission, doing God's work, crucially shaped foreign and imperial policy, acting as a kind of ideological framework in which to analyse events and make decisions. This, and recent studies on the Inquisition, have restored religion to a central place in discussions of Philip's reign.

1 The Inquisition and the Struggle Against Heresy

> **KEY ISSUES** What role did the Inquisition play in Philip's campaign against heresy? How have interpretations of the role of the Inquisition changed over the years? What were the consequences for Spain of this campaign against heresy?

a) The 'Protestant Panic'

Philip's reign began with an extraordinary wave of persecution against 'Lutheran' heretics. This was extraordinary because, almost uniquely amongst European states, the Protestant Reformation had not affected Spain. How can we explain the sudden emergence of Protestant cells in several Spanish cities? Although historians have demonstrated that there was indeed a small Protestant clique in a handful of Spanish cities in the 1550s, it's hard not to be sceptical. The 'Lutheran heretics' in Valladolid and Seville in 1558 were 'discovered' by the Holy Office of the Inquisition. But the organisation and its Inquisitor-General, Fernando de Valdes, had been suffering from a decline in influence during the preceding years, partly due to Spain's essentially stable religious situation. The sudden upsurge of heresy coincided with the accession of a new monarch, whose favour all members of court wished to gain. Whatever the reality of the situation, Valdes emphasised the threat of 'sedition and riot' and Philip and his regent in Spain, Juana, were convinced, it seems as much by this political threat as by concern for religious uniformity. A wave of persecution swept over Spain during 1557–1560. From May 1559, *autos de fé*, huge ritualised 'trials' and demonstrations of penance, were held in the main centres, attended by huge crowds and, after his return from the Netherlands, the King himself.

At these, some of the prisoners prepared to confess and do penance were publicly shamed and released, but many others, despite confessing, were committed for execution. The stubborn were burned alive. Although he professed himself to be uplifted by the ceremony and public exhibition of piety of the *autos de fé*, Philip did not personally attend the subsequent burnings of 77 heretics. The

A nineteenth-century French wood engraving, depicting an *auto de fé* from the sixteenth century. Note the ritualised processional nature of the event, and also the huge numbers of spectators. *Autos de fé* were major popular events, attended by thousands.

'Protestant panic' of 1557–1560 claimed nobles, members of the clergy and a number of respected and well-known Spanish humanists, including Agustin Cazalla, formerly a close associate of Emperor Charles; but although the crackdown has become one of the foundation stones of the 'Black Legend', Philip's regime was no more brutal in its pursuit of heretics and rebels than its counterparts in England or France during the same period.

Although the campaign subsided after 1561, Spanish religious policy had changed direction. *Limpieza* (purity of blood) statutes, excluding from Church institutions and certain monastic orders anyone of *converso* (converted Jewish) or *morisco* (converted Moslem) origins, had applied in many areas of the Spanish Church since the 1400s, but from the 1550s the number of institutions actually enforcing these regulations increased markedly, encouraged by Archbishop Siliceo's promotion of a *limpieza* statute in Toledo. Doctrinal uniformity was also enforced more rigorously. Before 1557, the Spanish Church accommodated a diversity of opinions, including mystics and

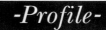

ST TERESA OF AVILA (1515–1582)

Perhaps Spain's most famous mystic and religious reformer, St Teresa of Avila courted controversy throughout her career with her ecstatic visions and her reforming mission. She founded the Observant order of the Discalced (shoeless) Carmelites in 1562 and in the succeeding years travelled the length and breadth of the country establishing daughter houses and preaching the reform of the religious life. By 1590, the Discalced Carmelites had established 81 priories and convents around Spain. St Teresa was an important writer on spirituality, and her *Life* became influential and popular – Philip II kept a copy by his bed. Her advocacy of reform set her firmly within the ranks of the Catholic Reformation, but her association with mystics like St John of the Cross provided her critics with ammunition for accusations of heresy. She was briefly investigated by the Seville Inquisition in 1576, primarily because of her *converso* antecedents, and her *Life* was only licensed for publication after Teresa's death. However, she enjoyed the protection of Philip II, which enabled her to escape persecution, and on her death the King had her papers and manuscripts moved to his personal library at the Escorial.

humanists. Whilst these were still to be found in the Spanish religious establishment after 1560 (for example the Carmelites St Teresa of Avila and St John of the Cross), they were much more guarded in their activities and were careful to cultivate the protection of powerful patrons. Furthermore, the power of the Inquisition meant that many humanists and theologians whose views had, in the past, strayed marginally from the orthodox line, became more circumspect. The theologian and poet, Luis de Leon, who himself fell foul of the Inquisition, talked of 'keeping silent out of fear'.[2]

Alongside the arrests, a raft of repressive measures was enacted. Castilian (later all Spanish) students studying abroad were recalled and an Index was created, monitored and enforced by the Inquisition, on which dangerous and heretical books were placed. These were forbidden to be printed in Spain or imported.

> 1 We order that no bookseller, book merchant or any other person of any state or condition may bring, smuggle, have or sell any book,

printed or unpublished work which has been prohibited by the principal office of the Inquisition in whatever language, form or material that
5 constitutes the book, under penalty of death, the loss of all goods and
the burning of the said books.
(*Decree establishing the Index, issued by Regent Juana, Sept 1558*).[3]

The Index was periodically updated and expanded (the 1583 edition
encompassed 2,315 titles), and eventually included works by many
prominent Spanish religious thinkers, along with European literary
luminaries such as Dante, Thomas More and Erasmus. The vernacu-
lar Bible was unreservedly banned.

b) The Anti-Heresy Campaign Assessed

Philip's anti-heresy measures have often been accused of closing off
Spain to the intellectual currents of the day and thereby retarding the
country culturally, but this is debateable. The Index proved impossible to enforce; it was the 1590s before Philip was able even to extend
the Inquisition's control over printed materials beyond Castile to the
rest of Spain. Given its limited resources, the Inquisition stood little
chance of effectively impeding the flow of banned books. Prohibited
texts continued to reach Spain from Italy, France, and the Low
Countries and with a little effort anyone with a taste for suspect literature and a modicum of resourcefulness could obtain them. Philip II's
own library in the Escorial contained numerous illegal works, and
Don Jose A. de Salas, a Castilian nobleman, managed despite the
restrictions of the Index to amass a substantial collection of 250
banned books.

Had early modern Castile been a police state with a substantial
apparatus for monitoring and apprehending lawbreakers, such a
repression might have been viable, but the Inquisition was seriously
over-worked and its duties were far more extensive than simply polic-
ing the statutes of 1558–59. Each tribunal consisted of three inquisitors and a support staff of variable size, but there were only 15
inquisitorial districts for the whole of Spain. Thus 45 inquisitors,
assisted by a host of largely unpaid subordinates, monitored the
orthodoxy of eight million people. Moreover, the Holy Office fulfilled
an educative role and was instrumental in enforcing the Tridentine
decrees (see pages 65–6). The bulk of its work after 1570 was inspec-
torial, monitoring orthodoxy and levels of ignorance among 'Old
Christian' (non-Jewish or Morisco) parishioners in rural Spain where
the majority of the people had little real understanding of either doctrine or the liturgy. Its limited budget (the Holy Office was never adequately funded and ran at an annual deficit) meant that its
hard-pressed staff could not possibly carry out this broad range of
duties. Consequently, they relied heavily upon *familiars* and *comisarios*
(locally-appointed, often unpaid officials, usually drawn from the

parish clergy) to maintain contact with local communities. The enthusiasm with which ordinary Spaniards sought appointment to these posts, and their readiness to denounce individuals during inquisitors' field trips suggests popular support for the Inquisition. In the Cuenca district, south-east of Madrid, 88 per cent of denunciations during the period 1561–1631 originated from the laity, which suggests that the small village communities of central Castile saw the Inquisition as a means of enforcing communal moral standards and acceptable religious behaviour.[4] In this way, the Holy Office, or at least its local agents, did reach remote communities, although inquisitorial inspections were infrequent, especially in remote rural areas. Thus, whilst we should not over-state the extent of the Inquisition's control over daily life in Spain, equally, as Sarah Nalle argues, the Inquisition was never 'marginal to the daily lives of Spaniards.'[5]

The Inquisition remained first and foremost a crown agency, staffed predominantly by legally trained priests and lawyers, and ultimately dependent upon royal favour and authority. The long-running saga of Archbishop Carranza of Toledo (see page 71) emphasises how often the Inquisition served political purposes or became embroiled in factional intrigues. Further energies were dissipated in 'turf wars' with other branches of the Church establishment. Under the leadership of a series of Dominican Inquisitor-Generals, the Inquisition fought a long campaign against the Franciscan and Jesuit orders, even citing Loyola's 'Spiritual Exercises' as heretical. The Inquisition was often resented as a tool of Castilianisation in Catalonia, Aragon and Valencia, where both the ecclesiastical and civil authorities protested that its activities were a breach of their '*fueros*' (provincial liberties). In Aragon, the Perez Affair (see pages 31–2) discredited the Inquisition, leading one official to complain that 'the lords and leading persons … wage war on the Holy Office.' Everywhere, critics denounced their reliance on anonymous informers and the use of torture and imprisonment without trial.

2 | The Counter-Reformation in Spain

> **KEY ISSUES** What was the condition of the Catholic Church in Spain at the time of Philip's accession? How, and how effectively, did Philip II attempt to reform the Spanish church?

a) The Spanish Church in 1560

The Spanish Church at the time of Philip's accession was in dire need of reform. Whilst educated Spaniards appear to have been knowledgeable and devout, the rural poor seem to have had little real Christian understanding. Contemporaries commented on the weakness of the Church's ministry in the remotest corners of the kingdom.

An inquisitor reported in 1572 that 'Galicia ... lacks the religion that there is in Old Castile, has no priests or lettered persons or impressive churches or people who are used to going to mass and hearing sermons ... They are superstitious and the benefices so poor that as a result there are not enough clergy'.[6] A Jesuit priest complained that, in Huelva, 'many live in caves, without priests or sacraments; so ignorant that some cannot make the sign of the cross; in their dress and way of life very like Indians'. In Catalonia, pre-Tridentine Catholicism 'was not governed by regular observance of the sacraments.'[7] Religion was a communal affair, serving the villagers' need for sacramental 'magic' to ease their daily struggle. Indeed, the nature of much popular religious practice and ritual in the early sixteenth century has persuaded many historians that 'over much of Spain, Christianity was still only a veneer'.[8] On St Joan's Day, Catalonian peasant girls used traditional charms and rituals to ensure that they would find partners, whilst in the mountains of Navarra, peasants sought to ensure good spring rains by dipping a statue of their patron saint (St Peter) in the local river. The state was conscious of the 'unsatisfactory reality of belief and practice among the Old Christian clergy and laity'[9] but despite the committed missionary efforts of the religious orders, notably the Jesuits and Franciscans, the campaign to raise standards of religious observance had been piecemeal for much of the sixteenth century.

Before the Catholic Reformation could remedy this, it first had to improve the quality of the priesthood, which was impoverished, poorly educated and morally compromised at the outset of Philip's reign. In Barcelona diocese, only 10 per cent of priests in 1549 were

THE SOCIETY OF JESUS (THE JESUITS)

The Jesuit order, founded by the Spanish soldier-priest, Ignatius de Loyola, was the vanguard of the Counter Reformation after 1540. Most active as missionaries in hostile environments, notably the Americas, the Far East and Protestant Europe, the Jesuits also played an important role in education and in spreading the Catholic Reformation to the remoter corners of Catholic countries. Philip employed the Jesuits to help spread Tridentine practices throughout his thinly populated and isolated kingdoms. However, after 1573 the next two Vicar-Generals of the Order (Mercurian, 1573–81 and Aquaviva, 1581–1615) were Italian, and this altered the Jesuits' relationship with the monarchy. Their traditional loyalty to the Pope, in the context of difficult relations between Spain and the Papacy, meant that the Jesuits were thereafter regarded with suspicion in Madrid.

resident, and the 1562 visitation (bishop's inspection) revealed that one in five possessed a mistress. However, the reform of the clergy required active and effective bishops. Although there were outstanding bishops in the Spanish church, they were thinly spread, and many regions had long been neglected. The visitation of the Catalonian town of Mediona in 1574 was the first for a century. Recognition of these structural weaknesses in the church lay behind the determined pressure exerted by Philip's representatives at Trent for the reform of clerical abuses to form a separate but important part of the decrees finally issued.

b) The Council of Trent and the Tridentine Decrees

The 'Catholic Reformation' of the second half of the sixteenth century arose from 'a yearning for an intense religious life, purified and disciplined by the hierarchy'.[10] In Spain, the teaching role of the Church expanded. Alongside this the State attempted to improve standards of discipline and education among the clergy. Seminaries were established and religious art flourished, as did several religious orders established in the first half of the century.

The institutional medium for this re-launching of Catholicism was a council of the whole Roman Catholic Church, convened by the Pope at the Italian city of Trent in 1546. The Council of Trent sat, on and off, for 18 years, and enjoyed enthusiastic support from Philip II. Some of Spain's finest theologians, intellectual titans like Domingo de Soto and Lainez, participated in the Council, and Spain's diplomatic and moral weight was instrumental in maintaining the impetus of the deliberations, which concluded, in the form of a series of decrees, in 1563.

However, Philip II and the Papacy squabbled over Philip's demand that the Pope accepted the secular ruler's authority over the episcopacy (bishops) in his territories. Although this quarrel laid the foundations for future disagreements between the Papacy and the Spanish Crown, Philip nonetheless promulgated the entire corpus of decrees in July 1564.

THE DECREES OF THE COUNCIL OF TRENT, 1563

The Tridentine decrees dealt systematically with catholic doctrine, the reform of abuses and the nature and structure of ecclesiastical authority. The most important features are listed below:

- Priests had to preach a weekly sermon
- Sunday schools should be established in every parish
- Transubstantiation was re-affirmed as central to Catholic doctrine. (This was the belief that the bread and wine in the com-

munion service miraculously turned into the body and blood of Christ as it was consumed, thus re-enacting Christ's sacrifice on the cross and purifying the sinner)
- The role of the sacraments in salvation was restated
- Parishioners would henceforth be expected to attend Mass weekly and take communion at Easter
- The confessional and the importance of penance were restated
- Bishops were instructed to set up seminaries for the training of priests in every diocese
- Priests were instructed to wear distinctive vestments
- The Latin Vulgate Bible was confirmed as the officially sanctioned version for use in Catholic worship

c) Reforms Undertaken by Philip II

Philip's personal commitment to religious reform was evident in the energy with which he promoted the Tridentine decrees within Spain. The Latin Vulgate Bible, and later the Roman Missal and Breviary (published in 1568 and 1570), were introduced. Seminaries were established across Spain, and a new archdiocese at Burgos and several new bishoprics were created. In an effort to provide the Spanish church with more dynamic leadership, Philip promoted a generation of educated, energetic bishops, men like Juan de Ribera, Archbishop of Valencia from 1568. Another, Gaspar de Quiroga, was made Archbishop of Toledo and Primate of the Spanish church in 1576. Working closely with the Inquisition and the religious orders, Quiroga set out uncompromising codes of conduct enforcing Tridentine standards upon the parish clergy. Similarly, considerable encouragement was given to those who sought to raise standards of discipline and piety in the religious orders, most famously St Teresa.

However, the Spanish Church was surprisingly unsupportive of the monarchy's reforming efforts, and Philip found the process of modernisation more difficult than he must have expected. Whilst Ribera in Valencia suppressed surplus feast days and irreverent rituals, and encouraged religious instruction and the wearing of vestments, elsewhere the campaign barely got off the ground. Many dioceses did not establish seminaries. Even the energetic Quiroga found that the Toledo diocesan clergy stubbornly resisted his efforts to do so, implausibly citing the poverty of the diocese (the richest in Europe!) as their reason. In the end only 20 seminaries were up and running by 1598. The clergy only gradually and reluctantly adopted Tridentine standards of education, behaviour and dress. Years later, the Mallorcan clergy were still resisting clerical vestments.

Attempts to expel non-Christian practices from everyday use in religious life met with only limited success. Confraternities (groups of laymen who organised religious services and charitable work) were encouraged by the authorities as a means of fostering devotion and discipline, and they met with some success. May festivals and St John's bonfires were banned, and plays, public meetings, business and games were prohibited inside churches. However, the state did not possess the resources to ensure nationwide compliance with these prohibitions. The problems encountered when the government attempted to ban bullfighting on holy days were symptomatic. Despite the support of the King (Philip hated bullfighting), the local clergy and elites often failed to enforce the ban and even bishops and inquisitors attended them. Philip himself could not entirely shake off medieval superstition. He assembled a huge collection of relics, which were deployed in his chapel to invoke the assistance of this or that saint.

Meanwhile, in the Netherlands, Philip promoted a root-and-branch reorganisation of the church in the 1560s, establishing 13 new bishoprics, funded by the reallocation of revenues from the existing four. Undoubtedly, this would have made the Dutch Church significantly more effective, but the project alienated the nobility and the existing Church establishment, whilst giving rise to fears that the Inquisition would be introduced in the wake of the reforms. Ultimately, the plan contributed to the collapse of trust between Philip and his Dutch subjects.

The implementation of Trent was reinforced by a redoubled effort from the missionary orders, and simultaneously the Inquisition diverted its energies away from the prosecution of heresy and towards the encouragement of religious orthodoxy amongst 'Old Christians', using visitations to monitor their morals and religious practices. Kamen has shown that the primary concerns of the Catalonian Inquisition, after the Protestant scare of 1557-60 had died down, were moral and disciplinary.

The Activities of the Inquisition in Barcelona, 1578–1635.[11]

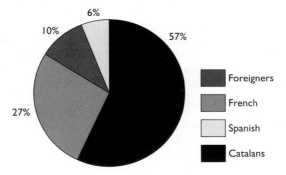

6%
10%
57%
27%

Foreigners

French

Spanish

Catalans

Table 1. Offenders, by Nationality.

Inquisition Discipline (i.e. officers of the Inquisition)	20%
Superstition	11%
Offences By Laity (e.g. anti-clericalism)	13%
Offences By Clergy (e.g. seduction, concubinage)	19%
Moral Control	15%
Sexual Offences (e.g. bigamy, bestiality)	20%
Horse Theft & Miscellaneous	2%

Table 2. Offences of 996 Catalans, by Type.

Years	Autos De Fé	Condemned	Moriscos	Moriscos as % Of Condemned
1550–1559	4	377	271	72%
1560–1569	4	420	368	88%

Table 3. The Activities of the Inquisition in Granada, 1550–1569.[12]

These local studies support Kamen's contention that the Inquisition, aside from one or two exceptional periods of activity against heresy or particularly 'dangerous' racial groups, was occupied mainly in monitoring 'Old Christian' morality and religious practices. Thus, as the Catholic Reformation advanced, the Inquisition evolved into 'a gigantic teaching machine'[13] and an instrument for social control.

Meanwhile efforts were made to improve the church fabric and to remove inappropriate images from churches, and both the clergy and the Inquisition sought to eradicate sexual offences, which were regarded as blaspheming the sacrament of marriage. In rural Spain, however, inquisitors adopted less rigorous standards than elsewhere, arguing that most of those arrested in rural areas were ignorant and uneducated, rather than heretics. Realistically, the parish clergy were probably more effective in disseminating the ideals of counter-reformation Catholicism, since they were permanently based in the community. The one-off, short sharp shock administered by an inquisitorial visitation was inevitably less effective.

d) The Consequences of Philip's Reforms

Did the efforts of the Counter Reformation church in Spain bear fruit? Despite recent research, it is difficult to be precise. Certainly the era witnessed a flourishing of Catholic culture; El Greco and Titian decorated the churches and cathedrals of Spain with spectacular devotional art. Equally, the Crown promoted highly educated and energetic bishops and the religious orders experienced a period of renewal. However, even in 1588, an inquisitorial report on the Catalonian chapter of the Augustinian order of friars reported:

1   [They] have no provincial chapters, ... no visiting inspectors and are not visited. They are not cloistered ... have almost no rule of obedience and go where they like. They have women in their houses. They give no account of their income. In some monasteries, they stopped performing
5   the masses and the ceremonies to which they were obliged by the terms of their foundation. They carried offensive weapons. They have no teachers to teach them grammar and so most of them are totally ignorant and cannot even read. They used to dance publicly with women. Some have been found guilty of very serious crimes, adultery, fornication, theft,
10   homicide, simony, enmity and ... of being friendly with bandits.[14]

The differences between the clergy and the laity were restated forcefully, and the priesthood's role in the daily life of the church was re-emphasised. A uniform formula for worship and doctrine was enforced, bringing remote regions fully into step with the Mother Church. Local saints were replaced with officially approved ones. But did this translate into a more effective ministry? Were the Spanish people 'christianised'? Here historians are the victims of their sources, for ordinary Spanish peasants left few records with which we can judge their beliefs. However, studies of inquisitorial records in Toledo and Cuenca suggest that levels of basic religious knowledge (measured by the ability to recite the Lord's Prayer, for example) rose sharply, from around 40 per cent before 1555 to around 82 per cent by 1600.[15] We must set this however against evidence suggesting that, especially in rural areas and remote corners of the country, many barely-Christian practices endured into the seventeenth century. One hundred years after Trent, a missionary in the remote Pyrenees reported that there was 'a very great need there to teach doctrine, because even the adults were like children in their knowledge and were ignorant of the most fundamental things'. Overall, historians paint a rather disappointing picture of the progress made by the Catholic Reformation by the end of Philip's reign, concluding that 'in the daily life of the nation ... the only immediate impact was made by the changes in public liturgy ... The external structure of the Church remained untouched.'[16]

3   Philip and the Papacy

> **KEY ISSUE**   Why were relations between Philip II and the Papacy so difficult?

Given Spain's importance in defending Catholicism against its enemies, we might expect Philip's relations with the Papacy to have been close. In fact, however, power politics intervened to undermine what ought to have been the central alliance around which Catholic Europe rallied its forces in the second half of the sixteenth century. In Italy the Pope, as the ruler of the Papal States, was a significant figure in Italian politics. However, Philip was ruler of Naples, Sicily, Sardinia and Milan, and closely allied to Tuscany and Genoa, and thus the dominant political influence in the peninsula. This caused problems. Philip began his reign at war with the Papacy, following Pope Paul IV's politically motivated excommunication of Philip. Although this was quickly resolved, relations remained difficult. Fearing that he would become a puppet of Spanish interests, the Pope constantly sought to give himself room for diplomatic manoeuvre by playing Spain off against the other great Catholic power, France. The weakness of late sixteenth century France and the reliance of Catholic Europe upon Spanish arms for its security against Ottoman and Protestant threats only made the Papacy more resentful of its dependence upon Philip.

Philip appreciated the need for good relations with Rome and his ambassador in Rome expended considerable effort and money to form a pro-Spanish party in the Vatican. Cardinals were showered with bribes and Spain frequently interfered in papal elections to ensure the victory of sympathetic candidates, although this ultimately backfired when, in 1592, the pro-French Clement VIII was elevated to the Holy See.

Further complications in the delicate relationship between Spain and Rome arose from Philip's insistence that he controlled the Spanish Church, from episcopal appointments to the publication of papal bulls and the implementation of the Tridentine reforms. Philip was entitled, under a concordat between the Spanish crown and the Papacy, to claim that 'in the rights that I have, and that my predecessors have handed down to me, there will be no change'. A series of conflicts over precedence resulted which poisoned the relationship between Spain and the Papacy. Lynch famously concluded that the state's control over the church was 'probably more complete in Spain than in any other part of Europe'.[17] Philip presented benefices to clergymen, bishops and archbishops, thereby ensuring his control over an enormous fund of patronage and, of course, over the kind of appointees preferred. He consequently received one-off 'first fruits' gifts from newly appointed bishops and abbots. He was also able to 'farm' the revenues of vacant bishoprics, a lucrative source of extra revenues. But Philip took his responsibilities seriously, dispatching commissions around Spain and his other imperial possessions to monitor the performance of the parish clergy and bishops. The Papacy's protests that 'His Majesty's ministers interfere too much in ecclesiastical jurisdiction' fell upon deaf ears.

Philip also blocked attempts to assert papal jurisdiction over heresy or other prosecutions involving churchmen, preferring the

Inquisition to deal with these issues within Spain. This led to a long and bitter battle over the trial of Archbishop Carranza of Toledo, arrested by the Inquisition in 1557. Carranza, a prominent religious thinker and formerly Philip's protégé, was swept up in the anti-Protestant fever at the start of the reign, but was primarily the victim of intrigues within the Spanish Church establishment, which resulted in an alliance between clerical rivals, the theologian Melchior Cano and Inquisitor-General Valdes, to destroy him. Arrested on the basis that his *Commentaries On the Christian Catechism* contained 'many propositions which are scandalous, rash and ill-sounding, others which savour of heresy, others which are erroneous and even some which are heretical',[18] Carranza was held for seven years by the Inquisition, although his innocence was abundantly clear to all except his jailers and Philip II. He became a political pawn, as Philip, determined to uphold the authority of the Inquisition, resisted the Pope's efforts to transfer the case to Rome until 1566. Even after Carranza had been transferred to the pope's jurisdiction, Philip's envoys stalled his acquittal for a further decade. In the end Carranza was finally acquitted in 1576, only to die 18 days later. Similarly, although Philip and the Papacy cooperated at the Council of Trent, Philip insisted on having the Tridentine decrees double-checked by his own canon lawyers before the Spanish crown proclaimed them in July 1564.

Philip and the Pope quarrelled over foreign policy too. The Spanish King was constantly hectored by the Pope to embark upon one crusade after another, against the Turks, against Elizabeth of England, against heresy in the Netherlands. But Philip, knowing full well that he, and not the Pope, would bear the costs of such an aggressive policy, resisted until the 1580s. Then, urged on by the Papacy, he laid plans for the conquest of England. Thereafter Philip often complained that, seeing that he was engaged upon God's work, he deserved more substantial support from the Pope. When, in the name of religion, Philip intervened in France in the 1590s, he was outraged to discover that the Pope was conspiring against him, working to obtain Henry IV's conversion and recognising him as the rightful ruler of France. He bitterly upbraided Sixtus V:

1 Nothing has surprised me more than to see Your Holiness ... leaving time for the heretics to take root in France, without even ordering that the Catholic partisans of 'the Bearnais' should separate from his cause. The Church is on the eve of losing one of its members; Christendom is
5 on the point of being set on fire by the united heretics. Italy runs the greatest danger, and in the presence of the enemy we look on and temporise! And the blame is put on me because, looking at those interests as if they were my own, I hasten to your Holiness as to a father whom I love and respect, and as a good son remind him of the duties of the
10 Holy See! But the greater my devotion the less I shall consent to your failing in your duty towards God and towards the Church... I shall insist on your setting to the task.[19]

The reality was that the Papacy feared a triumphant Spain, which would be dominant in Europe, and therefore trod a delicate line between supporting Europe's most ardent defender of Catholicism whilst avoiding becoming a Spanish client. Furthermore, in the crisis of the 1590s, the Papacy's cautious and flexible approach to the new, Protestant French King bore more tangible fruit than Philip's military solution. In 1593, Henry IV converted.

4 Analysis – 'Champion of Catholicism'?

> **KEY ISSUES** How effective was Philip II's religious policy? Can he be described as the 'Champion of Catholicism'?

Philip is often seen as the 'champion of Catholicism' in the late sixteenth century, and the evidence of his religious policy at home largely bears out this judgement, notwithstanding his tetchy relations with the Papacy. It is arguable, however, whether his championing of the cause of religion was successful. Some historians (e.g. Kamen) have concluded that Spain was barely more christianised by 1600 than it had been in 1500, for all the efforts of the King, the Inquisition and the Counter-Reformation. Others point to real progress in raising clerical standards and in countering the advance of Protestantism in Spain. However, against this must be set the treatment of perceived heretics, all too often merely humanists or harmless mystics. Equally, the persecution endured by the *moriscos* (see pages 41–3) and the enforcement of codes of '*limpieza*' amounted to an attempt to ethnically purify Spanish Catholicism and, even at the time, attracted criticism within and outside of Spain. The Jesuit political thinker Juan de Mariana condemned Philippine Spain's religious intolerance and rigidity, and proponents of the 'Black Legend' have, through the ages, echoed such denunciations. Motley wrote of the Inquisition that 'It taught the savages of India and America to shudder at the name of Christianity. The fear of its introduction froze the earlier heretics of Italy, France and Germany into orthodoxy... It condemned not deeds but thoughts... it arrested on suspicion, tortured till confession, and then punished by fire'.[20]

Such exaggerations and distortions have not gone unchallenged. Revisionist historians have re-evaluated Philip's religious policy, pointing out that, of the 40,000 or more 'heretics' investigated by the Inquisition under Philip II, only around 250 were executed. Instead, they offer us the more positive picture of a regime striving, certainly, to purify the nation, but also to educate and reform its morals and worship. It is, however, true that this positive appraisal glosses over the ruthless exclusion of the *moriscos* and *conversos* from membership of the 'religious community'. Indeed Netanyahu asserts, controversially, that the treatment of minorities in sixteenth century Spain foreshadowed later Nazi racial-religious persecution.[21] In at least one respect, the issue of alleged 'witchcraft', Spain displayed greater enlightenment than most of the rest of Europe, the Inquisition concluding in 1526 that there was little evidence of the existence of witches. Consequently, the witchcraze largely by-passed early modern Spain.

References

1 Letter from Philip II to Requesens, Spain's ambassador to Pope Pius V, 12th August 1566.
2 Cited in H. Kamen, *The Spanish Inquisition* (Phoenix, London, 1977), p. 217.
3 Taken from G. Woodward, *Philip II* (Longman, 1992), p. 106.
4 S. Nalle, 'Inquisitors, Priests and People During the Catholic Reformation in Spain' in *16th Century Studies* (1987), p. 576.
5 Kamen, *The Spanish Inquisition*, p. 257.
6 Cited in H. Kamen, *Inquisition and Society* (Berkeley, 1991), p. 199.
7 H. Kamen, *The Phoenix and The Flame* (Yale, 1997), p. 6.
8 Kamen, *Inquisition and Society*, p. 199.
9 A. D. Wright, *Catholicism in the Reigns of Philip II and Philip III* (Lewiston, 1991), p. 3.
10 Dominguez-Ortiz, *The Golden Age of Spain* (London, 1971), p. 201.
11 Kamen, *Inquisition and Society*, p. 259.
12 Taken from J. A. P. Jones, *Europe 1500–1600* (Nelson, London, 1997), p. 301.
13 J-P Dedieu, cited in H. Rawlings, 'The New History of the Spanish Inquisition' in *The Historian* 56 (1997), p. 32.
14 Cited in Kamen, *The Phoenix and the Flame* p. 71–2.
15 See Rawlings, 'The New History of the Spanish Inquisition' in *The Historian* 56 (1997), p. 32.
16 *Ibid.*, p. 431.
17 J. Lynch, *Early Habsburg Spain* (Oxford, 1986), p. 257.
18 Cano, cited in Kamen, *The Spanish Inquisition*, p. 161.
19 Letter from Philip II to Pope Sixtus V, 1589 in G. Woodward, *Philip II*, pp. 107–108.
20 J. L. Motley, *The Rise of the Dutch Republic* (London, 1951), p. 165.
21 See W. Makin, 'The Spanish Inquisition' in *History Review* (March 1997) for a very readable assessment of the main arguments in B. Netanyahu, *The Origins of the Inquisition in 15th Century Spain* (New York, 1995).

Summary Diagram

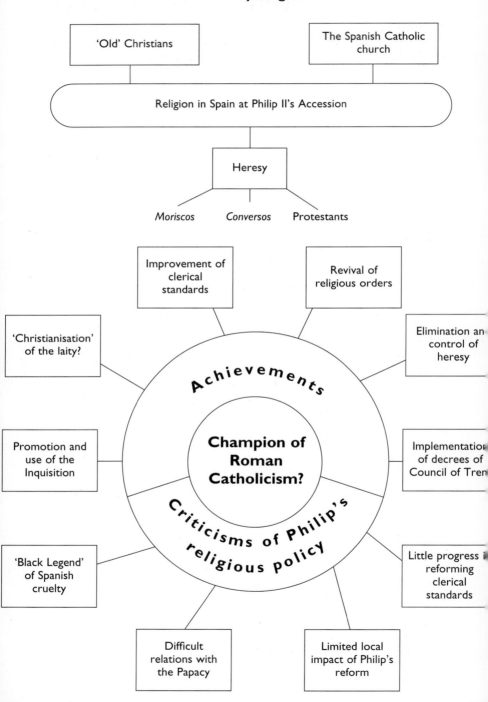

Working on Chapter 5

This chapter addresses the debate surrounding the nature of Philip II's religious policy, and your notes should enable you to engage in this debate. There are two key questions to consider:

1. Was Philippine religious policy primarily repressive, concentrating on the eradication of heresy, or was it more positive, attempting to promote a reformed Catholicism in line with the Council of Trent? (AIMS).
2. How successful was Philip in his efforts? (ACHIEVEMENTS).

Consider carefully the best way to organise your notes. The Summary Diagram above can be used as a basis for a pattern approach to your note-making. Alternatively, you might use a 'question approach'. This requires that you identify the key questions that make up the two larger issues.

An Example of a Question Approach to Note-Making on Religion

Why did Spain experience a 'Protestant Scare' during 1557–1560?
Who/what were 'conversos' and 'moriscos'?
Why were they regarded with suspicion in sixteenth-century Spain?
By what means did the Inquisition monitor and control heresy?
How effectively was heresy controlled in Philippine Spain?
In what ways have historians differed over the role of the Inquisition?
Were Spanish religious life and the Church in need of reform in 1555?
How and why did Philip II support the work of the Council of Trent?
How did Philip II and the Spanish church attempt to reform Spanish Catholicism after 1560?
How successful were Philip II's efforts to reform the Spanish Church?
Why were relations between Philip and the Papacy so difficult?
In what ways did this make Philip's efforts to champion Catholicism, within Spain and abroad, more difficult?

Having answered these questions in your notes, you should be able to cope with most structured questions, which will often take the form of two or more of these. Good notes on these issues should make it possible for you to address more substantial essay-style questions, like those below, with more confidence.

Answering essay questions on Chapter 5

Essays on Philip II and religion almost invariably address the issue of whether he could be described as a 'champion of Catholicism'. The questions below are pretty typical.

1. How far did Philip II live up to his title of 'The Most Catholic King'?
2. How far does the evidence of Philip II's domestic policy support his claim to be 'the Champion of Catholicism'?

Question 1 requires an assessment of Philip's foreign policy, as well as his management of religious matters within Spain and the empire. (For foreign policy, see chapters 7 and 8.) Question 2 is more narrowly focused, requiring only that you examine Philip's domestic religious policies. The first thing that you must do here is to consider what kind of question you have been set. The answers to this will determine the way you approach the task. Ask yourself the following questions.

a) Does this question focus equally on every aspect of the topic?
b) What are the boundaries of the question? For example, foreign policy is expressly excluded in question 2. Should we therefore, leave aside considerations of Philip's relations with the Papacy?
c) What is the analytical focus of the question? Is it about causation or the consequences of policy? Is it a comparitive question? Does it require assessment of success and failure, or offer an argument for you to agree with or challenge?

Having done this, you need to establish what key issues the essay requires you to incorporate into your answer. List these, in the form of sub-headings or questions. Now add to your list the essential factual points that relate to the headings you have chosen to include. By the time you have done this, you should have a fairly clear idea what you think of Philip's religious policy, but before you sit down to write the essay, jot down a brief (say, 50 word) 'conclusion', whilst the planning and thinking you have just done are still clear in your mind. This will ensure that, as you write, you always keep in mind the goal towards which you are steering the essay.

Source-based questions on Chapter 5

Source-based questions at AS and A Level sometimes ask you to evaluate statistical evidence, often in comparison with written sources. Study the picture on page 60, the chart and tables on pages 67 and 68, and the extract on page 69. Then answer the questions that follow.

a) Examine Chart 1 and Tables 2 and 3 on pages 67 and 68. What do they reveal about the priorities of the Inquisition in Spain? *(4 marks)*
b) Read the extract from the Inquisitor's visitation on page 69. Comment on the reliability and usefulness of his report. *(3 marks)*
c) Examine the French wood engraving of an *auto de fé* on page 60. How useful would this engraving be to an historian studying these events? *(3 marks)*
d) 'Marginal to the daily lives of Spaniards.' Using the sources, and your own

knowledge, how far do you agree with this assessment of the impact of the Spanish Inquisition upon Spanish life during Philip II's reign? *(10 marks)*

In answering d) above, always keep in mind that this question carries half the total marks available. You should therefore produce a thorough and carefully supported answer, which draws, as explicitly demanded, upon *both* the sources *and* your own knowledge. You have been given a historian's viewpoint, and are asked to agree or disagree with it, so the best approach is to treat it like a 'mini-essay'. Write a coherently argued answer to the question, using the sources as you go along to back up your points. When referring to the sources, identify them by letter, so as to make it clear that you have used them as requested.

The Problems of Empire – Finance and the Spanish Economy

6

POINTS TO CONSIDER

This chapter focuses primarily on the close relationship between finance and Philip's foreign policy. This relationship works in both directions. Philip's ability to wage war depended on the state of Spain's finances, but equally this was significantly affected by the spiralling costs of Philip's perpetual warfare. The other key issue of this chapter is the economic health of Spain during Philip's reign. After a century of steady growth, Spain's economy began to stagnate towards the end of the century. Explaining this and assessing the extent to which the Spanish economy had actually begun to decline by 1600, are the other key objectives of this chapter. Consider also the implications of these economic trends for Spanish society and the strength of the nation. This brings us back to the relationship between war and society, the economy and the state finances.

KEY DATES

1557 Philip's first declaration of bankruptcy.
1559 Treaty of Câteau-Cambrésis ends the Habsburg-Valois wars.
1560 Second 'unofficial' bankruptcy of the reign.
1571 Lepanto campaign costs 1 million ducats.
1572 Second Dutch Revolt begins. During the next 40 years, Spain spends 80 million ducats in the Netherlands.
1575 Philip declares his second official state bankruptcy.
1588 Armada, costing 10 million ducats, sails against England and is defeated.
1590 The *millones* tax is introduced, to pay for the war against England.
1596 Philip's third state bankruptcy is declared.

Fundamental to any assessment of the Spanish economy during Philip II's reign is the understanding that the empire, and indeed Spain itself, was not a single economic unit. Currencies, economic regulations and tariffs differed in each of Philip's possessions. Whereas Sicily, for example, remained essentially agrarian and feudal, other regions, notably the Netherlands, were highly urbanised and commercial. Within Spain itself, Aragon, agrarian in nature, faced the Mediterranean and was affected by climate, weather and harvest fluctuations, whereas Castile, especially the emerging cities of Seville and Cadiz, was Atlantic-focused and more sensitive to developments in international trade.[1] Even the Spanish currency was complex. The basic unit was the *maravedí*, but 400 *maravedís* made up one *escudo* and 375 made up one *ducat*, the main unit of Spanish state finance. Just to confuse matters further, American treasure was calculated in *pesos* (worth 1.2 ducats each). Such complications meant that devising 'economic policy' was immensely complicated. Indeed, given the limitations on the power of any sixteenth century government and bearing in mind Philip's admitted lack of flair for financial and economic management, it's arguable whether it was even possible to devise economic policy at all.

1 Finance

> **KEY ISSUES** What were Philip II's principal sources of revenue? How important to Philip's finances were imports of Indies bullion? Why, despite his great wealth, did Philip experience financial problems during his reign?

a) The Problem of Finance

The biggest single problem that Philip faced as ruler of the Spanish Empire was finance. The Spanish economy was not inherently strong, and its resources, human and material, were sparse, yet its imperial commitments were extensive. This meant that Philip constantly experienced difficulties in paying for his military and civil commitments, and it goes without saying that the provinces were reluctant to pay what Philip and Castile believed was their 'fair share'. The American colonies generated the great wealth of the annual bullion fleet, which gave Spain more hard cash to spend than any of her European rivals and enabled her to borrow heavily, but this should not obscure the fact that the economy of Spain itself was insufficient to maintain its empire for very long.

When Philip returned to Spain in 1559, he was shocked to discover the full extent of the financial crisis he'd inherited. Having been out of the country for several years, he'd assumed that Castile was richer than it proved to be. He wrote to Granvelle in the Netherlands, 'Apart from nearly all my revenues being sold or mortgaged, I owe very large sums of money and have need of very much more for the maintenance of my realms . . . I am greatly distressed to see the state in which things are'.[2] He shouldn't have been surprised. He himself, when regent of Spain during his father's reign, had resisted Charles I's continual demands for more money as prejudicial to the peninsula's economic well-being, and virtually his first significant decision as King in his own right, in 1557, had been to default on his debts and declare the state bankrupt, hardly an auspicious start. Faced with the situation he discovered on his return to Spain, he contemplated a second declaration of bankruptcy in 1560, but decided instead to operate an undeclared bankruptcy until he could stabilise the State's finances.

Even so, Philip II was the richest monarch in Europe. In 1556, his annual revenues totalled around 3.1 million ducats. But although the Spanish state had available to it numerous sources of revenue, it relied heavily on a handful of key income sources. These can roughly be divided into 'ordinary' and 'extraordinary' revenues.

b) Ordinary Revenues

The most important element of the ordinary revenues was the *alcabala*, a 10 per cent sales tax accounting for more than a quarter of Philip's total revenues in 1556. This was levied principally on the towns of Castile, and any alteration in the rate of collection required the approval of the Cortes, which strenuously resisted any such proposal. Since Charles's reign the cities represented in the Cortes had negotiated a fixed annual sum to replace the *alcabala*, called the *encabezamiento*, gathered in at the same time as the Crown's share of the tithe (the *tercias*). In the 1570s, Philip II forced through a significant increase in the *alcabala*, to 3,715,000 ducats per annum, despite determined resistance from the Cortes. However, these demands were excessive, and heavy shortfalls in the actual sums collected persuaded the King to reduce the level of the tax to a more manageable 2,715,000 ducats a year from 1577 onwards. Even this represented a significant increase on the totals raised in the 1550s, but it was clear that the ceiling of the *encabezamiento* had been reached.

Whilst it was difficult to raise the level of the *encabezamiento*, Philip was able to exploit other sources of revenue more effectively. The taxes upon the Granadan silk industry (the *seda*) and on the sale of salt (the *salinas*) were substantially increased. These raised impressive sums during the 1560s, but they also caused considerable political difficulties. The *seda*, which doubled during the 1560s, was one of the grievances contributing to the Moriscos Revolt in 1568 (see pages 41–3), and the yield declined noticeably after the suppression of the revolt and the dispersion of the *Morisco* population. Meanwhile, the *salinas*, which became a royal monopoly during Philip's reign, caused widespread hardship as it hit the poor, who could not do without salt, disproportionately hard.

Customs duties, especially those levied at Seville on the booming trade with the Indies, were a lucrative source of revenue, which expanded rapidly during the first half of the reign. This growth slowed in the 1580s, however, as the wars with England, France and the Netherlands disrupted trade. Finally, rents from Crown lands raised a negligible sum, which declined further as a proportion of the total during Philip's reign, due to the sale of substantial royal estates.

c) Extraordinary Revenues

Extraordinary revenues were potentially considerable, but were, by definition, irregular. The most substantial source of extraordinary revenue was the *servicio*, a one-off tax that required Cortes approval before collection. The burden of the *servicio* fell heavily on the middle and lower classes, since the clergy and nobility were exempt. Consequently, although the Castilian Cortes granted *servicios* on six occasions during Philip's reign, several requests were rejected, and on such occasions Philip's demands were met with angry protests.

However, the Cortes did show some understanding of the Crown's financial problems, and in 1590 the deputies agreed to the levy of a one-off tax on essentials like meat, oil and wine, called the *millones*. This was designed to raise eight million ducats over six years, to help pay for Philip's wars against England, France and the Dutch, but it was deeply unpopular and the receipts from the *alcabala* fell during the same period. The extension of the *millones* in 1596 sparked widespread protests and the cumulative effect of increased taxation at a time of economic dislocation due to war and poor harvests contributed to the collapse of the Castilian economy in the final years of Philip's reign. Whilst Castile bore the brunt of such one-off measures, other parts of the empire were affected too. The 'Hundredth Penny', levied in the Netherlands in 1569, faced similar opposition when it was extended in 1571.

Although exempt from regular taxation and the *servicio*, the Spanish Church did not escape the grasp of the Treasury. Clerical taxation expanded considerably under Philip II, becoming an increasing proportion of his revenues. The *tithe* had fallen into Crown hands during the middle ages, and it yielded a million ducats per year by the end of the reign. Taxes on the incomes of bishoprics, the exploitation of the income of vacant sees and the seizure of the estates of the military orders brought in hundreds of thousands of ducats more each year. Finally, the Pope authorised the Spanish Crown to collect the 'Three Graces', the *cruzada*, the *subsidio* and the *excusado*, which brought in a further 1.4 million ducats a year. Altogether Church taxation provided Philip with as much money as the *alcabala* by the 1590s. Devout as he was, Philip did not spend this money on the advancement of the Faith within Spain. Indeed, the Inquisition, a Crown agency first and foremost, was forced to be self-financing and was perpetually short of cash.

When he was particularly hard-pressed Philip resorted to more desperate measures to raise short-term cash. The sale of noble titles and crown offices did not generally raise significant sums, although in the build-up to the Armada campaign in the 1580s, large numbers were sold. The sale of common lands (*baldíos*) and royal jurisdictions (*senoríos*) could be lucrative, although the consequent alienation of

Crown authority and the strengthening of noble power in the localities was a heavy price to pay for the ready cash raised.

Despite all of these sources of revenue, Philip would have experienced considerably greater financial problems had it not been for the annual bullion shipments from the Indies, which rose steadily throughout the century and reached their peak towards the end of his reign, thanks in large measure to the opening of the silver mines at Potosi in Bolivia and at Zacatecas in Mexico. Total Spanish imports of bullion trebled between 1556 and 1598.

Period	Total (to nearest 100,000 ducats)
1556–1565	23.9 million ducats
1586–1595	70.8 million

Table 1 Spanish Imports of Bullion from the Indies during Philip II's Reign

The Crown was entitled to one fifth of the value of all precious metals and stones mined in the Americas (the *Quinto*) and this, together with the customs revenues at Seville and the income from other taxes in the colonies, brought in around 64 million ducats during the reign. The arrival each spring of the treasure fleet proved time and again to be a lifeline, as the bullion it carried could be set against Philip's debts to enable him to raise new loans and finance his continual wars.

Theoretically, Philip should have been able to raise further revenues from the other parts of the *monarquia*, especially wealthy regions such as Lombardy and the Netherlands, but the provinces resisted all attempts to make them contribute to the costs of defending the empire. Aragon contributed just five *servicios* during the reign, and largely evaded payment of regular taxes to the Crown, hiding behind its *fueros*. Philip's Italian possessions contributed to the costs of defending the Mediterranean against Turkish and Barbary threats; the Lepanto campaign, for example, was substantially financed by contributions from Philip's Italian provinces and allies. But generally Philip's Italian subjects were reluctant to finance his needs elsewhere. Philip's attempts to tax the Netherlands illustrate the difficulties he experienced. During the first decade of the reign, the Dutch contributed around 4.5 million ducats to the imperial treasury, but the 'Hundredth Penny', a one-off tax levied in 1569, was only grudgingly paid and Philip's decision to impose two permanent sales taxes (the 'Tenth' and 'Twentieth' Pennies) in the Netherlands was deeply resented, especially as it was primarily designed to finance the Spanish armies that occupied the Netherlands at the time. The Dutch Revolt of 1572 was partially a protest against this taxation, and resulted in a heavy fall in revenues from the province, together with a spectacular and ruinous increase in military spending.

Philip never managed to persuade the outlying regions of the

		1559	1572/3	1588	1598/9
Income	**Alcabala**	.89	1.28	2.75	2.9
	Servicios/Millones	.4	.4	.4	3.07
	Trade Taxes	.69	2.16	2.37	2.56
	Three Graces	.36	1.2	1.47	1.44
	Indies	.38	.8	2.0	2.6
	Casuals	.28	.56	.5	.3
	TOTAL	**3.0**	**6.4**	**9.49**	**12.87**
	Index (1559 = 100)	*100*	*213*	*316*	*429*
Spending	**Juros (Interest)**	1.49	2.75	3.5	4.63
	Govt and Court	.7	.8	.86	.8
	Flanders	–	1.85	2.73	3.45
	Defence of Spain	.74	1.1	3.4	3.4
	TOTAL	**2.93**	**6.5**	**10.49**	**12.28**
	Index (1559 = 100)	*100*	*222*	*358*	*419*

Table 2 State Finances: (Millions of Ducats)[4]

empire to contribute their share of taxation. In vain did he argue that 'all are in my charge and since in the defence of one all are preserved it is just that I should call on all'.[3] Consequently, the burden of financing the policies of Philip's Spain was borne disproportionately by Castile, whose taxation burden rose by around 430 per cent between 1559 and 1598. In 1592, when Philip's commitments were at their most intense, the hard-pressed towns of Castile were milked of 10 million ducats, but this was more than they could reasonably afford. Little wonder then that the Castilian economy entered a long period of decline in the 1590s.

d) Spending

Philip's perpetual inability to balance his budget, despite increasing threefold his revenues, primarily resulted from the fact that he spent virtually his whole reign at war. Moreover, the cost of waging war in the sixteenth century accelerated rapidly as new, expensive technology became available. The Armada fleet of 1588, although no larger than the Lepanto fleet in 1571, boasted eight or nine times its firepower, which increased its powder and shot requirements accordingly. Furthermore, it was entirely paid for by Spain, the Pope failing to support an enterprise he had urged for years. Since war was by far the biggest single area of state expenditure, this was a disastrous combination of factors.

Philip began his reign at war with France, and by the time peace had been achieved in the Habsburg-Valois conflict, he was already being forced to confront the Turks in the Mediterranean. The reconstruction of the Spanish navy after Djerba was immensely costly and the victory at Lepanto cost the crown 1 million ducats, although Philip was able to use the anticipated costs of Spain's involvement in the campaign to persuade Pius V to revive the 'Three Graces', which had been suspended during the 1560s. Parker has consequently played down the cost of the Lepanto campaign, arguing that Spain's annually 'recurring costs ... represented about 46 per cent of Philip II's share of the expenses of the Lepanto campaign ... Lepanto was not so much an unusual burden as a redirection of resources.'[5]

However, by the time that Philip had fought the Turks to a stalemate in the 1570s, he was embroiled in the Netherlands. The Army of Flanders grew from a garrison force in 1560 to an army of 67,000 in 1572, and it remained an immense drain on state finances for the rest of the reign, costing an estimated 80 million ducats over 40 years. During the 1580s, Philip was drawn into France's internal conflicts, subsidising the Catholic League and increasingly intervening on their behalf, and alongside the escalating conflict with England this placed the state under insupportable financial strain. By 1587, Spain was maintaining around 100,000 soldiers throughout the empire, and the Armada of 1588 alone cost 10 million ducats, making it necessary to levy the *millones*. More than any other single factor, the ongoing military expenses of maintaining the empire were responsible for Philip's three declarations of bankruptcy. Moreover, the substantial costs of billeting and recruitment were borne by the *communes* of Castile, especially those situated on the coast near the embarkation ports for the troops.

Despite attempts to economise in other areas, there was remarkably little slack to take in. Court expenditure was in fact relatively low. Philip did not have expensive personal tastes, and his court, although large, was fastidious and restrained. His artistic patronage and his interest in architecture accounted for his greatest personal costs, but although the Escorial palace cost about five million ducats, this was spread over 20 years and did not form a significant part of the crown's multiplying debt.

Early modern government was, by later standards, inexpensive to maintain. Officials' salaries were not impressive, although an acknowledged element of administrative corruption oiled the wheels of government and ensured office-holders an income. However, the sales of office and of *senorios* alienated other sources of revenue in lieu of salaries. There were significant costs involved in protecting Spain's coastline against piracy, especially during the 1560s and 70s, when North African pirates regularly raided Spain's Mediterranean coast. These areas were often neglected in favour of higher-profile projects, as Philip's officials in coastal areas complained: 'There are no horses, no weapons, nor anyone who knows how to handle them'.

Most frustratingly for the King, the need to service the Crown's spiralling debt was a huge drain on the Treasury. By the 1590s, when the
debt had grown to 87 million ducats (three times what it had been in
1555), interest payments on the state debt totalled 4.6 million ducats
a year, half of the total state revenues.

e) Analysis

As Table 2 on page 83 illustrates, for most of his reign Philip's spending outstripped his income. Consequently he was forced to resort to
borrowing on a grand scale. Only the Indies bullion enabled Philip to
meet the interest payments on a succession of increasingly huge
loans, raised by the sale of *juros* (long or medium term interest bearing state bonds) to domestic and foreign bankers, mainly in Genoa.
When *juros* were insufficient to meet the state's demand for cash,
Philip took out *asientos* (short-term loans, guaranteed to be paid, at
high rates of interest, at a specified date). These were highly lucrative
to the lender and ruinous to the state, but Philip had little choice but
to resort to *asientos* at times.

Philip's reliance upon 'deficit finance' to sustain his imperial commitments was ultimately disastrous. On three occasions during the
reign, he was unable even to meet his interest payments and was
forced to declare bankruptcy, in 1557 (largely a legacy from his
father's long-running wars with France), in 1575 and in 1596.
Additionally, in 1560, he rescheduled payments on his debts so as to
meet his immediate financial needs. Each of these crises can be
directly linked to soaring military expenditure. In 1573, Juan de
Ovando, the President of the Council of Finance, presented Philip
with a 'Memorial' containing a detailed assessment of the state of
royal finances. He pointed out forcefully that Philip had a debt of 74
million ducats but an income of only 5.6 million, and argued that
only radical steps would enable the King to regain control of his
finances. Ovando recommended cancelling Crown *juros* and increasing the *encabezamiento* by 2.5 million ducats, but these proposals pro-
voked a storm of protest in the Cortes. In the end, Philip suspended
debt payments in 1575 in a vain attempt to escape the clutches of his
Genoese bankers. The consequences of this declaration of bankruptcy were mixed. In the short run, Philip could reschedule or
cancel his debts, although he failed to break his dependence upon
the Genoese banking houses. However, short-term benefits were out-
weighed by the damage done to his credit and the impact bankruptcy
had upon future borrowing, which was often at a higher rate of
interest. The results for Philip's imperial policies were disastrous.
During a period of bankruptcy it was virtually impossible for the King
to spend any money, even if he had it. Consequently, after the 1575
declaration of bankruptcy, the Army of Flanders went unpaid for
more than a year, resulting in a series of ruinous mutinies and the

sack of Antwerp, which in turn created an irresistible groundswell of support for the Dutch rebels, forcing Spain to conclude a humiliating truce. A further attempt to break the Genoese hold on his finances in 1596 had similar results.

By the end of his reign, Philip had accumulated 87 million ducats of debt. Despite his determined exploitation of every source of revenue available to him, and the annual windfall of the Indies bullion, Spain was insolvent. The King cannot escape responsibility for this, since he signally failed to develop an effective strategy for managing the complexities of Royal finance. Even he was painfully aware of his deficiencies in this respect, admitting:

> I cannot tell a good memorial on the subject from a bad one, and I do not wish to break my brains trying to comprehend something which I do not understand now nor have ever understood in all my days.[6]

2 The Economy

> **KEY ISSUE** Why did the Spanish economy stagnate during the reign of Philip II?

a) Population

Spain's population, in keeping with general European trends, experienced steady growth during the sixteenth century, peaking at approximately 8 million around 1580 (although James Casey has recently argued that this figure is too high, preferring 6,632,000 in 1591).[7] The period of most rapid expansion was the mid sixteenth century, New Castile's population expanding by 78 per cent in the 70 years to 1591. Seville, the focal point of the Indies trade, more than doubled in size to a city of 24,000 households by 1590, and possessed 130,000 residents by the early seventeenth century, making it one of the largest cities in Europe. Other important commercial cities flourished, notably Cadiz, Seville's partner port in the Indies trade. Madrid grew too, benefiting from becoming Philip II's capital.

However, by the 1580s, population growth had slowed, and the 1590s marked the start of a long decline in some regions of Spain. Why was this? Spain's wars drained the country of thousands of young men each year, and emigration to the Americas drew away perhaps 200,000 of the more ambitious and enterprising during the sixteenth century. More significantly, in the 1590s epidemics and harvest failures resulted in dreadful, although localised, mortality crises that abruptly halted population growth, reversing it in many regions. Old Castile was affected particularly severely. The 1598-9 outbreak killed 12,000 of Segovia's population of 28,000, and Toledo, Valladolid and Madrid were all affected. One notable long-term trend was the depopulation of rural areas, as the peasants of Galicia and Asturias migrated to the booming cities of New Castile. There was also substantial migration from the kingdom of Aragon towards wealthier Castile. By the end of Philip's reign, Castile's share of the total population of Spain had risen to 81 per cent, while Aragon, Catalonia and Valencia could muster a mere 13.5 per cent.

b) Agriculture

These population crises were worsened by long-term structural weaknesses in Spanish agriculture, which meant that Spain could not feed its people adequately even in a good year. Spanish agriculture has always battled against the peninsula's climate and terrain and the sixteenth century was no exception. The climate was hot, dry and arid in the South and on the central plateau, and warm and wetter along the northern coasts. Owing to this, and the relatively mountainous and elevated nature of much of the country, perhaps only 40 per cent of Spain's terrain was cultivable but, even so, a surprising amount of land was left untilled, partially because archaic fallow practices required that only half, or even as little as a third, of the land was sown each year. Yields were low, even by the standards of the day, and there was little variation or experimentation in crops (rice, for example was not widely in use until the following century). Consequently, Spain struggled to feed her growing population as the century unfolded.

Even during the first half of the century, a relatively successful time for Spanish farmers, population growth seems to have generally been outstripping increases in food production. However, recent studies have shown that this relative prosperity was almost entirely the result of increasing the amount of land under cultivation, often at the expense of pasture traditionally used by the *Mesta* (the guild of sheep drovers, which possessed enormous influence in economic life), whose flocks declined throughout the era. Even so, huge tracts of land remained under-used (some critics estimated that two-thirds of Andalucia was waste) despite a systematic effort to break-up the *baldios* (common lands) and sell them off to more entrepreneurial farmers. From around 1570, agricultural yields, already amongst the lowest in Western Europe, started to fall dramatically. In 1578, Juan de Arrieta noted that 'the land is becoming exhausted and the fields are not as productive as they once were'.[8] Spain became increasingly dependent upon imports, generally from Sicily and Southern Italy but also from the Baltic, to compensate for her inefficiency, even during good years. The situation deteriorated further in the 1590s. The onset of a meteorological crisis across Europe, the so-called 'little ice age', found Spain's rural economy ill equipped to cope, and a combination of high taxes and rents, under-investment and poor climatic conditions drove farmers into poverty and ultimately off the land altogether.

Whilst the decade after 1589 was unquestionably exceptionally bad for weather, modern historians largely accept David Vassberg's judgement that the failure of Spanish agriculture was primarily structural, the result of 'man-made institutions that were inefficient, and that did not permit the proper utilisation of resources'.[9] Agricultural techniques remained very backward, and even established farming techniques were applied inconsistently. Consequently, the crisis of the 1590s hit arable and pastoral farming simultaneously. The government had hitherto failed to recognise the depth of Spain's agrarian crisis, responding to demands from the Cortes for interest rate reductions only in the 1570s. But in the 1590s the pressing nature of the situation forced the state to ban the seizure of peasants' ploughs or crops in lieu of debt-interest or rent payments. This wasn't enough to prevent the purchase by wealthy bourgeoisie of a lot of peasant holdings, and the consequent depopulation of the countryside.

c) Industry

Historians often underestimate Spain's level of industrial activity during the sixteenth century. Huge quantities of iron were mined in the North; Old Castile possessed a strong woollen industry, centred on towns like Segovia, and supplied with raw wool by the herds of the *Mesta;* alum, mercury and salt were all important export products; and Valencia and Granada possessed prosperous leather and silk industries, in which the Moriscos were prominent. Furthermore, the influx of bullion from the New World was, by 1556, creating a wealthy elite, who might potentially provide a domestic market for manufactured luxury goods. Additionally, Spain possessed valuable foreign and imperial markets. Nonetheless Spain's industry was sparse, relative to that in France or the Netherlands, and it suffered during Philip's reign from a lack of investment and the continued strength of the guild system. Only modern industries, like armaments or printing, were able to evade the restrictive practices of the guilds, but even here the failure of the Spanish elites to invest in industrial enterprises left Spanish industry slow to modernise, providing opportunities for foreign entrepreneurs to penetrate Spanish markets.

Philip II's reign witnessed the steady decline of traditional industries, as falling woollen and textile production in Segovia, Toledo and Cordoba demonstrates. This had a knock-on effect for the ports that traditionally carried this trade. Burgos declined as the wool exports to Flanders fell away during the Dutch war. One crucial failing was the preference amongst wool merchants for exporting 'raw', unfinished wool. As early as 1557, the Venetian ambassador noted that Spanish merchants sold too much of Spain's wool abroad unworked 'and then come to fetch from these countries cloth to wear and tapestries'. This growing dependence on imported finished, manufactured wool products, often from the same Flemish towns that were engaged in a bitter independence struggle against Spain, was very damaging to domestic manufactures. Government measures to encourage the retention within Spain of wool clip for use by Spanish artisans were only partially effective. The shipbuilding industry, especially in Portugal, remained buoyant, thanks largely to increased state orders in the 1560s and 1580s. However, the leather and silk industries of the South were irremediably damaged by the state's repression of the Moriscos (see pages 41–3).

It was not all doom and gloom. Seville, the nexus of the Indies trade, boomed, but a worrying sign of the weakness of Spanish manufacturing was the quantity of foreign goods imported by Spanish merchants for re-export to the Indies, including arms, manufactured goods, tools and luxury items. These products were often available from Spanish producers, but the merchants preferred to import cheaper, higher quality goods from abroad, encouraged by the government's decision in 1566 to allow Spanish merchants to export bullion. In effect, this allowed Spanish merchants to use the profits of the New World trade to buy in foreign manufactured goods rather than seek out domestic producers, but their preference may also have been influenced by the difficulties of transporting goods around the peninsula, due to the appalling roads and the tolls and internal customs barriers between Castile, Andalucia and Aragon. In effect, Seville became a European port, serving the general European economy, and dominated by foreign merchants rather than Spaniards.

By 1600, the pattern had been established whereby Spain exported raw materials and imported finished manufactured goods. This resulted in a net outflow of capital from Spain, which was exacerbated by the country's growing dependence on foreign supplies of food, notably wheat and (almost incredibly) fish. The balance of trade deficit that resulted drew out of Spain the proceeds of empire.

d) Trade and the Colonies

Historically, the lifeblood of Spanish commerce was the wool trade, based on the herds of the *Mesta*, the textile towns of Old Castile and the commercial links to Flanders and Northern Europe. However, the late sixteenth century witnessed the start of a long period of decline, due primarily to the Dutch Revolt and the failure of the Spanish industry to modernise. Instead, the Crown relied increasingly upon the prosperity of the constantly expanding colonial trade. Spain supplied her overseas possessions with a steady stream of manufactured goods: arms, Granadan silk, Catalan cotton and Castilian textiles. However, Seville's growing community of foreign merchants ensured that a high proportion of these exported goods were from other European countries. Critics railed against this 'senseless subjection to foreigners', but little could be done to prevent it unless the Spanish economy could meet the demands of the wealthy Indies colonists for manufactures.

Although the merchant convoys returned to Spain with growing quantities of spices, hides, cochineal and sugar, the most important cargo was gold and silver bullion. The New World bullion steadily rose in value as the century progressed, peaking in the final years of Philip II's reign, and between 1503 and 1660 185,000 kilos of gold and almost 17 million kilos of silver reached Seville.[10] However, the impact of the bullion was a rather mixed blessing. It enabled Spain to offset the unfavourable trade balance with the rest of Europe, but the result was that the once-only bonanza of the New World bullion was frittered away to pay for her failing economy. Likewise, the deployment of the bullion as a means of guaranteeing and paying off loans placed Spain at the mercy of international financiers. Without it, however, Philip would have been unable to pursue his policy objectives at all.

Worse still, the importation of such huge quantities of gold and silver contributed to inflation, although the extent to which the price rise of the second half of the century can be entirely explained thus has come under challenge in recent years. Earl J. Hamilton suggested in the 1930s that the correlation between the influx of New World bullion into Spain and the acceleration of prices was so close that there had to be a causal relationship.[11] Contemporaries felt so too. Towards the end of the century, the *arbitristas* (a school of Spanish economic theorists who recommended economic reform) blamed the influx of silver from the Indies for the decay of Spain's trade with other European nations, arguing that 'where money is scarcer than in Spain, bread, wine, cloth and labour are worth much less'.[12]

ı It is likewise an error to suppose that in good politics the wealth of a kingdom is increased or diminished because the quantity of money in circulation is larger or smaller. Since money is only an instrument of exchange, a small circulation has as good an effect as a large one ...
5 *Censos* are the plague and ruin of Spain. For the sweetness of the sure profit from *censos* the merchant leaves his trading, the artisan his employment, the peasant his farming, the shepherd his flock; and the noble sells his lands so as to exchange the one hundred they bring in for the five hundred the *juro* brings ... Wealth has been and still is riding
10 upon the wind in the form of papers and contracts, *censos* and bills of exchange, money and silver and gold, instead of in goods that fructify and attract to themselves riches from abroad, thus sustaining our people at home. We see, then, that the reason why there is no money, gold or silver in Spain is because there is too much, and Spain is poor
15 because she is rich.[13]

Inflation was clearly a problem towards the end of Philip II's reign, a constant theme of diarists, municipal authorities and Cortes deputies. In 1567, the city of Barcelona raised the wages of its employees, complaining that 'every article of human need is incomparably more expensive than it has ever been'.[14] (Wages seem generally to have kept pace with the 2.5 per cent average annual inflation rate during the period.) However, Hamilton's viewpoint has been challenged by historians like Cipolla and Vilar, who point out that much of the Indies bullion arriving in Seville was immediately re-exported to Italy, Flanders and Germany to cover the interest on the state's loans, and another large proportion went into the pockets of foreign merchants in Seville, who exported it to pay for the goods that they supplied to the Indies. The explanation for the inflation that afflicted Spain (and, indeed, Europe generally) towards the end of the sixteenth century may lie in a combination of factors: imports of bullion, the rising population outstripping food production, accelerating government spending and declining domestic manufactures forcing consumers to purchase goods at greater expense from abroad.

3 Conclusion

> **KEY ISSUE** Had Spain begun to decline economically by the end of Philip II's reign?

It appears that the economic and financial roots of the later decline of Spain were laid during the reign of Philip II. Economic activity declined significantly, Spanish manufactures proved incapable of beating off foreign competition and a debt of nearly 90 million ducats saddled the nation with an impossible burden. Spaniards were quick to grasp the extent of the problem. The *arbitrista* Mercado observed bitterly that 'the debit of Castile in European countries has become greater than its credit' and the Cortes of Castile in 1594 accounted for the difficulties being experienced in gathering taxation by arguing that 'the kingdom is wasted and destroyed, for there is hardly a man in it that enjoys any fortune or credit'. The *arbitristas* were merely the most articulate and sophisticated of the doomsayers predicting the decline of Spain, although they fixed upon a variety of explanations. In 1600, Cellorigo concluded: 'Henceforward we can only expect shortages of everything, because of the lack of people to work in the fields and in the manufactures that the kingdom needs',[15] and Justus Lipsius informed Spain ironically in 1603 that 'the New World, conquered by you, has conquered you in its turn'.[16] Whatever their explanations, their pessimistic assessment was borne out by the collapse of Spain as a Great Power in the century that followed.

References

1 See A. Dominguez-Ortiz, *The Golden Age Of Spain* (London, 1971), p. 190.
2 Cited in H. Kamen, *Philip of Spain* (Yale, 1997), p. 87.
3 Cited in G. Woodward *Philip II* (Longman, 1992), p. 28.
4 Adapted from I. A. A. Thompson, *War and Government in Habsburg Spain* (London, 1976), p. 288.
5 G. Parker, 'Lepanto The Costs Of Victory' in *Spain And The Netherlands* (Collins, 1979), p. 131–3.

6 Cited in Woodward, *Philip II*, p. 38.
7 See J. Casey, *Early Modern Spain: A Social History* (Routledge, 1999), p. 21.
8 J. Casey 'Spain – A Failed Transition' in P. Clark, *The European Crisis of the 1590s* (London, 1985), p. 212.
9 D. Vassberg, cited in H. Kamen, *Golden Age Spain* (Macmillan, 1988), p. 28.
10 E. J. Hamilton, cited in Dominguez-Ortiz, *The Golden Age Of Spain* (London, 1971) p. 297.
11 See E. J. Hamilton, *American Treasure And The Price Revolution In Spain* (Cambridge, Mass., 1934).
12 Azpilcueta, cited in Casey, *Early Modern Spain*, p. 69.
13 Cellorigo, cited in Woodward, *Philip II*, p. 105.
14 Cited in Dominguez-Ortiz, *The Golden Age Of Spain*, p. 195.
15 Cited in J. H. Elliott, *Imperial Spain* (Penguin, 1963), p. 298.
16 Cited in J. H. Elliott, *The Old World And The New* (Cambridge, 1972), p. 63.

Summary Diagram on Economy and Finance

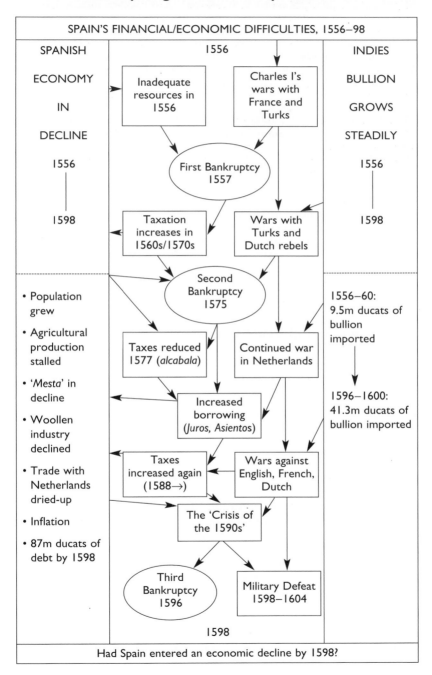

SPAIN'S FINANCIAL/ECONOMIC DIFFICULTIES, 1556–98

SPANISH ECONOMY IN DECLINE

1556

|

1598

INDIES BULLION GROWS STEADILY

1556

1598

1556

Inadequate resources in 1556

Charles I's wars with France and Turks

First Bankruptcy 1557

Taxation increases in 1560s/1570s

Wars with Turks and Dutch rebels

Second Bankruptcy 1575

- Population grew
- Agricultural production stalled
- 'Mesta' in decline
- Woollen industry declined
- Trade with Netherlands dried-up
- Inflation
- 87m ducats of debt by 1598

Taxes reduced 1577 (alcabala)

Continued war in Netherlands

Increased borrowing (Juros, Asientos)

Taxes increased again (1588→)

Wars against English, French, Dutch

The 'Crisis of the 1590s'

Third Bankruptcy 1596

Military Defeat 1598–1604

1556–60: 9.5m ducats of bullion imported

1596–1600: 41.3m ducats of bullion imported

1598

Had Spain entered an economic decline by 1598?

Working on Chapter 6

Financial and economic history can be difficult to get to grips with, but it is central to any understanding of Philip II's success and failure, and you need to compile clear, uncomplicated notes, especially on his financial problems. One useful way to organise your basic factual notes on Philip's state finances would be in the form of a table.

Source of Revenue	Explanation. (Simple Summary)	Value To Philip II/Importance
e.g. Alcabala	...	...

Philip's expenditure is less complex. War and the interest payments on the state debt accounted for a large portion of his spending. Brief notes, with examples, should suffice here. You will need to consider the ways in which the economic condition of Spain affected Philip's ability to raise taxes and the taxation regime affected the Spanish economy. Write a brief analytical conclusion. Finally, you must ensure that you are able to discuss the ways in which Philip's foreign commitments and the political problems he experienced in governing the empire affected (and were affected by) his financial situation.

Answering Essay Questions on Chapter 6

Essay questions on finance and the economy are quite common, so you must ensure that you are prepared to answer a question like one of those below.

1. Why, despite imports of bullion from the Indies, did Philip II so often find himself in financial difficulties?
2. To what extent was the rule of Philip II at home and abroad affected by Spain's economic and financial problems?

Question 1 above is an example of an 'explanatory' question, requiring that you produce a series of reasons why Philip II experienced financial difficulties. You need here to show that you are aware of a range of different issues, and a good place to start is by constructing a list of between four and six reasons, each of which can be expanded into a full paragraph in your essay. Obviously you must discuss the importance of the bullion, but your answer might also explore Philip's problems in raising revenue from other sources, his enormous and rapidly growing expenditure, and the structural weaknesses of the Spanish economy that restricted his ability to tax more heavily. A good answer would consider also relevant political factors, Philip's imperial policy and his own inability to handle matters of state finance. When you have constructed your list, you should consider which are the most significant factors. At this point remember that your essay should contain, as well as a range of points, an argument, encapsulated in your conclusion, leaving the examiner with a clear understanding of your views on the question.

7 Foreign Policy 1556–1584

POINTS TO CONSIDER

Although Philip II's conduct of foreign affairs was at times shrewd and skilful, at others it was clumsy and disastrous, and success and failure seem to have been concentrated into particular periods of Philip's reign. This chapter focuses on the period of Philip's greatest foreign policy successes. Victories over the Ottoman Turks in the Mediterranean brought to an end a long period of Turkish advances. The resulting stalemate in the Mediterranean might be seen as a kind of success for Spanish arms. The acquisition of Portugal in 1580 was perhaps Philip's greatest foreign policy achievement. If we set these achievements alongside Philip's success in neutralising England and France before the 1580s, can we regard Philippine foreign policy before 1584 as successful?

KEY DATES

1557	Victory over France at St Quentin.
1559	Treaty of Câteau-Cambrésis with France.
1560	Defeat of Spanish fleet by Turks at Djerba.
1565	Siege of Malta. Ottomans defeated by Spanish and Knights of St John.
1566	Death of Suleiman the Magnificent.
1567	Incident at St Juan de Ulloa between English raiders and Spanish navy.
1568	First Netherlands Revolt is crushed by Alva.
1568–70	Moriscos Revolt.
1571	Holy League formed against the Turks. Battle of Lepanto (Spanish victory). Ridolfi Plot against Elizabeth.
1573	Spanish recapture Tunis (briefly). Turks capture Cyprus.
1578	Battle of Alcazarquivir, at which King Sebastian of Portugal dies.
1580	Philip invades Portugal and claims the throne.
1581	Lasting truce signed between Turks and Philip.

Philip inherited his father's foreign policy in tatters. Defeated in Germany, stalemated in the long-running and costly war with France and under assault from Ottoman forces in the Mediterranean, Charles I had only the English alliance, forged through Philip's marriage to Mary Tudor, to cling on to by 1556. Philip therefore had little time to consider his options, but he responded to the manifold threats to his empire with considerable skill. By 1559, he had defeated the Franco-Papal alliance that faced him at his accession. Moreover, the division of the empire had divested Spain of any responsibility for events in Germany. On the other hand, he had been forced to issue a declaration of state bankruptcy in 1557, the death of Mary Tudor in November 1558 had terminated the English alliance, and the Turks were once again threatening Spanish interests in the Mediterranean. Only with the Peace of Câteau-Cambrésis in 1559 was Philip able to establish the boundaries of his own foreign policy.

1 The Mediterranean and the Turks

> **KEY ISSUE** How successfully did Philip II deal with the Ottoman threat in the Mediterranean?

a) The Struggle for the Mediterranean

Although there is much debate over the motives of Philip's foreign policy (see Chapter 8), it would appear that he saw himself, at least from time to time, as the 'Champion of Catholicism', and so he regarded it as his religious duty to resist the advances of Islam and the Turks. However, there is little doubt that Philip also appreciated the *political* necessity of resisting Ottoman expansion in the Mediterranean. Spain possessed vital strategic and commercial interests in the region, not to mention the territories of Sicily and Naples, and a number of North African outposts that appeared vulnerable to attack from the Turks and their allies, the Barbary corsairs (pirates based in fortified ports along the North African coastline). The advances of the Turks had been virtually unchecked since the 1520s, and the 1560s saw the climax in the titanic struggle between the two pre-eminent powers of sixteenth century Europe.

From the outset of Suleiman the Magnificent's reign, the capture of Belgrade (1521) and Rhodes (1522) signalled the Sultan's intention to expand the Ottoman Empire into central Europe and the Mediterranean. From this time forwards, Ottoman armies threatened Habsburg Austria, and the fall of Hungary in 1526 brought them to the very gates of Vienna. Meanwhile, in the Mediterranean, an alliance with the Barbary corsairs, commanded by the great Barbarossa, brought Moslem fleets into the Western Mediterranean, where they threatened the shipping lanes connecting Spain to her Italian possessions. The fall of Tripoli in 1551 raised the possibility of an Ottoman-dominated empire extending across North Africa as far as Morocco. As Philip ascended the Spanish throne the Turks threatened Tunis. Consequently, as soon as he could make peace with France, Philip turned his attention to the challenge of Suleiman's seemingly unstoppable Mediterranean advance.

However, the first attempt to stem the Moslem tide ended in disaster. In 1560, Philip dispatched an invasion force of 47 galleys and

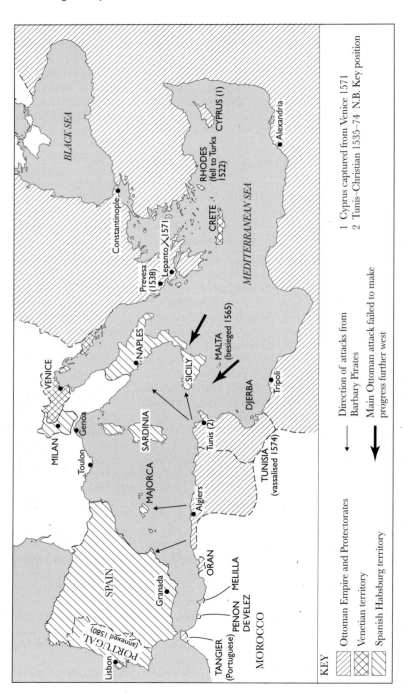

The Ottoman-Habsburg Struggle In The Mediterranean 1556–1581.

12,000 men under the command of the Genoese admiral Doria to retake Tripoli. The Spanish established an advance camp on the island of Djerba, whence they hoped to launch the assault. Unfortunately, they were surprised here on 12th May by a Turkish fleet. The troops fled in panic into the galleys but were caught before they reached open water. Virtually the entire Spanish invasion force was captured, with the loss of 28 galleys and 10,000 men. This unmitigated disaster forced Philip to embark on the construction of a new, modern fleet. Whilst the rebuilding programme advanced he had to rely for naval defence upon the fleets of his Italian allies, Genoa and Florence, and the Knights of St John, who operated out of Malta. These resources could not adequately protect the Spanish coast against the raids of the Barbary corsairs, aided, it was believed, by traitors amongst the Morisco population. Naples endured the humiliation of a blockade in 1561. The rebuilt Spanish fleet suffered a setback in 1562, when it was savaged by a sudden fierce storm off the Balearic Islands, but the progress of the naval build-up was indicated by the success in 1563 of an expedition in relief of the besieged North African outpost of Oran, which defeated the Barbary pirates. Following this in 1564, Philip's Captain General of the Sea, Don Garcia de Toledo led the new fleet in a successful expedition against Peñon de Velez, a notorious corsair base. The table below shows the extent of the Spanish rebuilding programme, and the extensive contribution of Philip's Italian possessions to the imperial navy in the Mediterranean.

Perhaps the turning point of the Ottoman-Spanish conflict arrived in 1565, when Suleiman launched a full-scale invasion of the strategically pivotal island of Malta. Malta, situated halfway between Spanish-owned Sicily and hotly contested Tunis, controlled the passage from the Eastern Mediterranean to the West. Suleiman's forces, numbering more than 30,000, landed on 18th May 1565 and besieged the capital of the island (modern day Valetta). The garrison of a thou-

Squadron	1562	1567	Oct 1571	1574	1576	1577
Spanish: in Spain	7	10	18	37?	40?	33
Spanish: in Italy	7	15	14	14	*	*
Naples	8	14	33	54	44	32
Sicily	10	10	10	22	22	14
Doria (Genoese)	12	11	11	12	12	12
Others	11	19	10	16	16	11
TOTAL FLEET	55	79	96	155	134	102

* Incorporated into Spanish squadrons

Table 1: The Spanish Navy in the Mediterranean (Numbers of Galleys)[1]

sand Knights of St John and around 8,000 Maltese peasants held out heroically for four months until the viceroy of Sicily, Don Garcia de Toledo, could muster together sufficient ships and soldiers to mount a rescue mission. Don Garcia's caution was much criticised by contemporaries, but was well merited. An over-hasty rescue mission would have invited disaster, but the appearance of the Spanish fleet off Malta in September forced the Ottomans to raise the siege and retreat. It was a momentous victory, and the Spanish contribution to the ultimate defeat of the Ottoman fleet was vital. Suleiman's armies were shown to be beatable, and the linchpin of the empire's forward defences was saved. With Suleiman's death the following year, Philip gained breathing space while the Sultan's successor, Selim, consolidated his position at the head of the empire. Unfortunately, Philip was unable to use this time to strengthen his defences in the region or to exploit the Turks' temporary disarray, as within months of one another in 1568 both the Dutch and the Moriscos in Granada rose in rebellion. By the time the uprisings had been quelled, two years later, the opportunity had slipped away.

In July 1570, the Turks launched a new assault in the Mediterranean, attacking Venetian Cyprus. This Venetian outpost in the heart of the Ottoman-dominated Eastern Mediterranean had long been a target of Turkish designs, and Spain's problems in Granada provided the sultan with an irresistible opportunity. At the same time the corsair King of Algiers, Euldj Ali, seized Tunis. However, the energetic crusading Pope Pius V assembled a Holy League, including Papal, Venetian and Spanish forces to resist the Turks, with the intention of relieving Cyprus. Spain was to provide half the forces and finances of the alliance, with Venice providing one third and the Papacy one sixth, but in reality much of Philip's contribution was from his Italian possessions and allies. Even so, the cost to the Spanish treasury was considerable, calculated at 1 million ducats. The whole force totalled some 300 ships, carrying around 80,000 men, commanded by Philip's energetic and charismatic half-brother Don John, and inevitably an enormous force took several months to assemble. Consequently, by the time the fleet gathered at Naples in August 1571, the final Venetian stronghold on Cyprus, Famagusta, had fallen. Don John decided therefore to seek out the Ottoman fleet and give battle, and subsequently he headed for the Greek coast near Corfu, where the Ottoman fleet, at least the equal of the Christian force, was anchored. On the morning of 7th October 1571, the two naval forces met at Lepanto and the League won a crushing victory. The Ottoman admiral, Ali Pasha, was killed, 117 Ottoman ships were captured and dozens more sunk. Only one wing of the Turkish force escaped the carnage. However, on the Christian side losses were heavy, with around 9,000 soldiers killed, although only 20 ships were lost. Christian Europe was delighted.

'The Adoration Of The Name Of Jesus (Allegory of the Holy League)' by El Greco (National Gallery, London). The victory at Lepanto became a popular subject for painters in Spain during the 1570s. El Greco's painting was an attempt to curry favour with the King, who did not like the painter's work, by praising his triumph. The King is shown piously at prayer, receiving the blessing of Heaven for his efforts.

One Venetian historian claimed:

> The Turks are not insuperable as we had previously believed them to be … As the beginning of this war was for us a time of sunset leaving us in perpetual night, the courage of these men has bestowed upon us the most beautiful and joyous day.[2]

The morale value of the victory should not be underestimated. As Braudel observes:

> The victory can be seen as the end of a period of profound depression, the end of a genuine inferiority complex on the part of Christendom and a no less real Turkish supremacy. The Christian victory had halted progress towards a future that promised to be very bleak indeed.[3]

Philip and Spain, who had provided the bulk of the fleet and whose empire had largely financed the expedition, took great credit from the victory. Titian was commissioned to paint a huge allegorical canvas commemorating 'Spain Coming to the Aid of Religion' and El Greco offered his own tribute, in his 'Allegory of the Holy League' (see page 101). Even Elizabeth I, showing unusual Christian solidarity, sent a message of congratulations to the victors.

b) After Lepanto – Stalemate

Lepanto was the greatest victory of Christian Europe over the forces of Islam since Granada, 80 years earlier, but its long-term strategic significance was less impressive. It was too late in the year to follow up the victory with an immediate offensive against the Ottoman Empire itself, and by 1572, cracks were beginning to appear in the Holy League. The Venetians wanted to use the success as a springboard to recapture Cyprus, and the Pope hoped to take the offensive into Ottoman waters, demanding a crusade against the infidel. Philip had other ideas, however. He did not share Pius V's crusading enthusiasm and was primarily concerned with the security of the Spanish empire, preferring 'to gain some benefit for my own subjects and states from this league and all its expenses rather than employ them in so risky an undertaking as a distant expedition in the Levant'. Accordingly, he ordered Don John to resist any attempts to engage the Turks in the Eastern Mediterranean, nearer to their reinforcements. In May 1572, Pius V died, and the hiatus in Papal policy that accompanied the election of his successor allowed Philip to delay the dispatch of a promised Holy League expedition to Turkey. In March 1573, the Venetians withdrew from the League in disgust, signing a separate peace with the Turks that renounced Venetian claims to Cyprus in return for the reopening of their trade relations with the Ottoman Empire. Spain's recapture, the same year, of Tunis, seems to bear out the wisdom of Philip's limited and sensible strategy, although the difficulty of defending such an exposed outpost of Spanish power in the Mediterranean was amply illustrated by the fall of the city to the Turks the following July. By this date, Philip was deeply embroiled in the Netherlands Revolt and on the verge of bankruptcy so there could be no response to this Turkish success. Tunis, and any thoughts of an anti-Islamic crusade in the Mediterranean, were abandoned. For their part, the Ottomans had their own reasons for seeking peace with Spain in the 1570s. The death of the Shah of Persia, on the Ottomans' eastern borders, opened up new opportunities for expansion in the East, and the empire's increasingly over-stretched military commitments dictated a policy of disengagement with Spain. Both sides were receptive to truce proposals in 1578 and this temporary cease-fire became a permanent treaty of peace in 1581.

Any argument that Philip blindly pursued a self-appointed role as the champion of Catholicism seems untenable in the face of his negotiation of a succession of truces with the Turks after 1578. The adoption of a policy of détente reflected the limited, defensive nature of much of Philip's foreign policy in the Mediterranean, which had never been aggressive and had always sought merely to preserve the vital strategic interests of the Spanish Empire. Modern analysts readily concede that this was wise and well judged, but at the time his readiness to parley with the Turks was regarded by Catholic Europe and the Papacy in particular as a kind of betrayal. Nonetheless, it cannot be denied that, at the time, Philip had more pressing concerns, and that an ideologically-driven foreign policy, fighting Christianity's battles against Islam, was neither in Philip's dynastic interests, nor in the strategic best interests of the Spanish Empire. Peace was clearly the most desirable policy in the circumstances, and Philip's ability to abandon the straightjacket of religious ideology (for once) is commendable in one so devout.

2 Relations With France Before 1584

> **KEY ISSUE** How did Spain benefit from the civil wars in France?

At the time of his accession, Philip was at war with France. The prolonged Habsburg-Valois conflict had effectively bankrupted both participants, but this did not prevent Henry II from launching a fresh offensive against Spain in 1557, assisted in Italy by the anti-Spanish Pope Paul IV. The Papal armies were defeated by the Duke of Alva, whilst Philip launched a retaliatory campaign in Northern France and Flanders, which culminated in victory at St Quentin in August 1557. The Constable of France, Montmorency, was among the dozens of senior French noblemen taken. The capture of so many of the elite of the French nobility, and the subsequent victory at Gravelines forced France to sue for peace, although not before Henry II had seized Calais from Philip's ally, England. Negotiations opened in October 1558 and culminated in the peace of Câteau-Cambrésis on 3rd April 1559. Câteau-Cambrésis represented a victory for Spain. France was forced to accept Spain's possession of Milan and Naples and Henry II ceded Piedmont to the Duke of Savoy, a Spanish ally, effectively excluding France from Italy for the next 240 years. By way of compensation, Henry retained Metz, Verdun and Toul, captured from the Holy Roman Empire in 1552, and Calais, but the terms of the treaty were bitterly resented by many Frenchmen. In order to cement the treaty, Philip married Henry II's daughter Elisabeth de Valois. This diplomatic union would prove a vital link between the two crowns during the next decade, as France tumbled into civil war and Philip faced the threat of the Ottomans in the Mediterranean.

However, France remained a problem for Philip. At first, his neighbour's disintegration into civil war granted Philip breathing space in which to address his other problems, but as the civil strife in France deepened, Spain found herself inevitably drawn into it. A small Spanish force assisted the French crown against its rebellious Protestant subjects in 1563 and 1569. However, the death of Elisabeth in 1568 meant the end of the familial link between the two dynasties, and the intervention, firstly of Coligny and then of Anjou, in the Netherlands revolt threatened vital strategic interests of the Spanish crown and could not be ignored. Equally worrying, as the French religious wars progressed, was the growing power of Henry of Bourbon, the Protestant cousin of the French King and ruler of the autonomous (self-governing) Pyrenean kingdom of Navarre. Huguenots (French Protestants) sheltering in Navarre from Catholic persecution elsewhere in France raided across the border into Spanish Navarra and Catalonia, bringing with them their heretical ideas. The inability of the Inquisition to contain the spread of Protestantism via this route led Philip to conclude that he had to prevent Henry of Navarre from becoming King of France.

3 Relations with England to 1584

> **KEY ISSUE** Why, and with what success, did Philip II maintain peaceful relations with England before 1585?

During the first decade of Philip's reign, relations between Spain and England were cordial and business-like. Both Philip and Elizabeth were cautious rulers, who sought to avoid being drawn into a war with each other, but there were too many divergent interests for the two rulers to remain on peaceful terms indefinitely. However, although ultimately the two countries went to war, we should steer clear of the assumption that this was pre-ordained.

At the behest of his father, who wished to draw England into the Habsburg camp, Philip married Mary Tudor, Queen of England, in 1554, and consequently during the early years of his reign, he enjoyed cooperative and friendly relations with the English regime. The

English people did not trust his motives, however, and Mary was unable to carry the nation with her when England entered the renewed Habsburg-Valois wars on the side of Spain in 1557. English troops did fight alongside Spaniards at the battle of St Quentin in August 1557, which secured victory for Spain, but the loss of Calais the following spring meant that England gained little from her involvement. After Mary's death in 1558 and the accession of Elizabeth, a Protestant, relations became more complicated, but remained peaceful, even after England's failure to regain Calais in the Treaty of Câteau-Cambrésis. Philip, vainly and one supposes not entirely sincerely, proposed marriage to Elizabeth but despite her refusal, only his efforts during the 1560s prevented the Pope from excommunicating the English queen. Philip's motives for protecting Elizabeth were entirely related to the power politics of Europe's dynasties. Elizabeth's sole realistic challenger for the throne of England was Mary Stuart, the Catholic Queen of Scotland, who was related by marriage to the Valois Kings of France. Therefore, despite her Catholicism, Mary was unacceptable to Spain as Queen of England while she retained close links with her French relatives. Elizabeth, on the other hand, was Philip's sister-in-law, for whom he had developed a healthy respect during his time in England. Consequently, Philip overlooked Elizabeth's heresy, and persevered with the traditional Anglo-Spanish alliance.

However, this position became increasingly impossible to maintain. During the 1560s, a series of trade disputes over the Indies damaged relations between the two monarchs. By the Treaty of Tordesillas the Pope had, in 1494, divided the New World between Portugal and Spain, and since then all trade with Spanish colonies had been routed through Seville in order to ensure payment of fees to the Crown of Castile. However, English merchants and privateers sought entry to this lucrative market. Sir John Hawkins transported West African slaves to the Indies, supplying (at a price) the labour needs of the colonists, but his activities breached both the Treaty of Tordesillas and Spain's restrictive trade laws. In September 1567, Hawkins's flotilla of English merchant-privateers was intercepted at San Juan de Ulloa and destroyed by Spanish ships. English protests smacked of hypocrisy given that, when not trading illegally with Spanish colonists, English ships raided and pillaged their settlements along the Caribbean coast. Such police action by the Spanish authorities was, in fact, entirely legitimate. Nonetheless, Elizabeth responded in 1568 by seizing a shipment of bullion headed for the Spanish forces in the Netherlands, which, due to bad weather and pirate activity, was forced to put in at Plymouth. The English ambassador in Madrid was recalled and Spain's ambassador, de Spes, confined to his embassy in London. Trade between the two kingdoms was abruptly halted, which only served to penalise the many merchants on both sides engaged in legal trade with one another. Normal trading relations were only restored in 1573, through the Convention of Nijmegen.

In 1568, a second issue arose to disturb relations between Elizabeth and Philip. The flight of Mary, Queen of Scots from her rebellious subjects to her cousin south of the border precipitated a fresh crisis, since Elizabeth, unsure of how to deal with such a loose cannon at large in her kingdom, arrested her, imprisoning her for the next 20 years in a succession of fortresses. Mary's predicament aroused great excitement across Catholic Europe, and Philip was drawn into a series of conspiracies to liberate Mary and set her on her cousin's throne. Initially, Philip's interest in such affairs was cool and cautious. However, by 1570 Philip was considering various options for the invasion of England and the overthrow of Elizabeth. His ambassador in England was certainly involved in the failed plot devised by the Florentine merchant and Papal agent Ridolfi in 1571. This followed the disastrous uprising by the Catholic 'Northern Earls' in 1569, which had sought to install Mary as Queen, but which resulted in the disgrace and execution of the most powerful Catholic noblemen in England. Letters to the Duke of Alva, then Spain's Governor of the Netherlands, indicate that Philip was keen to exploit any opportunity that might arise from the uprising. Alva, however, recognised the dangers of fishing in Elizabeth's troubled waters and found various ways of avoiding acting. Undaunted, Philip persisted with attempts to destabilise the English Crown. The Throckmorton Plot of 1587 certainly had Spanish assistance, and this convinced Elizabeth that she could no longer ignore the evidence of collusion between Mary and Philip. Mary was executed in 1588.

The realisation of her vulnerability to Spanish attack led Elizabeth to adopt a dual policy. On the one hand, England diplomatically courted both France and Spain during the 1570s, in the hope of counter-balancing, with French aid, the threat from Philip. On the other hand, Elizabeth financed and encouraged an undeclared privateering war on Spain's colonies. English sailors launched a series of expeditions to the Americas during the 1570s, establishing Raleigh's colony in Virginia, and Drake's circumnavigation of the globe was partially financed with the profits from pillaging Spanish colonies and shipping. English ships fought alongside those of Philip's Portuguese rival Dom Antonio in the Battle of Terceira, off the Azores. Meanwhile, Philip, encouraged by the Pope, explored other possibilities for the removal of the 'Protestant Jezebel', assisting an unsuccessful invasion by English Catholics of Ireland in 1580. This undeclared war culminated in Philip's decree, issued in May 1585, authorising the seizure of English merchant shipping in Spanish ports.

Probably the most damaging issue was, however, the English response to the war in the Netherlands between Philip and his rebellious Dutch subjects (see Chapter 5). The outbreak of the Netherlands Revolt in 1566 complicated Anglo-Spanish relations considerably. The

Protestant Dutch could rely on the sympathies of most Englishmen, although Elizabeth's position on the issue was at first rather ambiguous, partially because, as a divinely appointed monarch, she had little sympathy for rebels. Nonetheless, as the conflict in the Netherlands deepened, it became increasingly clear to Elizabeth that a rebel Protestant regime was preferable to an altogether more powerful Spanish presence, which would present a threat to England's security. Consequently, she allowed English Protestant 'volunteers' to help the Dutch, and she funnelled funds the way of William of Orange. This was bound to cause conflict eventually, and the series of victories won by the Duke of Parma between 1581 and 1585, strengthened the hand of the 'War Party' in Elizabeth's Privy Council. The assassination of William of Orange in 1584, followed by the fall in 1585 of Antwerp, finally forced Elizabeth to come off the fence. Philip's seizure of English ships in Spanish ports only served to silence the moderate, 'anti-war' party in Elizabeth's court, and in August 1585 Elizabeth and the rebel 'United Provinces' concluded the Treaty of Nonsuch, which committed England to the defence of the rebel provinces against Spain. England and Spain, after maintaining a respectful, if increasingly fraught peace for 25 years, slipped inexorably into war.

4 Portugal – The Reunification of Hispania

> **KEY ISSUES** Why did Philip incorporate Portugal into his empire in 1580? How, and how successfully, did he pursue the unification of Spain and Portugal?

The Spanish and Portuguese monarchies had long-standing familial connections, which were expressed quite explicitly in the person of Philip II, whose mother was Isabel of Portugal. Philip was served throughout his lifetime by Portuguese, most notably, Ruy Gomes da Silva, the Prince of Eboli, who was one of his closest advisors and friends. Quite aside from his legitimate dynastic rights as the son of a princess of the House of Portugal, Philip harboured the ambition to reunite the Iberian Peninsula, recreating the *Hispania* that had last existed under the Romans 1,000 years earlier. Portugal also possessed important colonies in Brazil and the Far East, as well as one of the largest navies afloat. It is perhaps understandable then that Philip had coveted Portugal for some time before he finally got his chance to seize the country in 1580. His opportunity arose because of a fortunate turn of events, but his exploitation of the opportunity was a master-class in the art of power politics.

In 1578 the young Portuguese King Sebastian, Philip's rather unbalanced nephew, sallied forth into the deserts of Morocco to challenge the Ottoman domination of the region. Sadly, his expedition ended in disaster at the battle of Alcazarquivir (4th August 1578), where Sebastian and the flower of the Portuguese nobility were wiped out. The young King was unmarried and the last of his family, so the succession passed to his uncle, Henry, ageing, sick and a cardinal of the Roman Catholic Church, hardly a long-term solution! As Henry's health declined, a succession crisis arose. Who would be the next King when Henry died? The principal candidates were Catarina, Duchess of Braganza, who claimed descent from Manuel the Fortunate (a fifteenth century Portuguese King); Dom Antonio, the Prior of Crato, illegitimate son of one of Sebastian's uncles, whose dissolute and spendthrift lifestyle won him the support of the commons; and Philip of Spain. Technically Philip's claim was a strong one, but he did not rely solely upon his legitimacy. During 1579, he dispatched one of his closest advisors, the Portuguese, Don Cristobal de Moura, to cultivate the merchants of Lisbon, who identified themselves closely with the fortunes of Spain anyway, through enormous loans advanced to the Crown. He also won over many of the Portuguese nobles, partly by ransoming them from captivity in Morocco. By this mixture of diplomacy and bribery, he assembled a strong party in Portugal. Meanwhile, he recalled the Duke of Alva from disgrace to command a strong invasion force, and positioned his army near the border, awaiting the opportunity to march into Portugal and claim his throne.

In January 1580, Henry died, and the proclamation of Dom Antonio as King by the people of Lisbon gave Philip the signal he had awaited. Henry had failed to nominate a successor before his death and the Portuguese *Cortes* was divided between the nobility, who supported Philip, and the lesser gentry, backing Catarina. Philip's grant of substantial estates and the title of Constable to the Duke of Braganza persuaded Catarina to withdraw from the contest.. On 13 June, Alva's disciplined Spanish *tercios* crossed the Portuguese border. Against Spain's superior military force, Dom Antonio's 'populist party' could only offer the support of the Lisbon populace and the possession of the city's arsenal. A brief and brilliant campaign by Alva resulted in the fall of Lisbon and the flight of Dom Antonio in August. Dom Antonio established a government-in-exile in the Azores, but a subsequent attempt by the pretender, supported by French ships, to seize Sao Miguel, the main island of the group, was defeated by a Spanish fleet under Santa Cruz in July 1582. Dom Antonio's base at the smaller island of Terceira remained a threat to Spain's Atlantic shipping and the following year Santa Cruz launched a successful amphibious assault, which secured the island and ended the threat posed by Dom Antonio.

In December 1580, Philip entered Lisbon, promising to respect the privileges and rights of his Portuguese subjects. Portugal's governmental institutions were retained and her traditions were respected. Portugal retained administrative control over her overseas possessions and her trade continued to pass through Lisbon, carried in her own ships. In effect, Portugal remained an entirely separate kingdom from

Spain, connected solely by the accident of possessing the same monarch. For the next three years Philip governed his empire from the palace at Lisbon, where, in an unusual display of tact, he trimmed his beard in the Portuguese manner, conducted business in the language and adopted Portuguese fashions at court. In many respects, Philip demonstrated in the Portuguese affair the sort of political acuity, decisiveness and energy that we do not usually associate with him. As he pithily expressed it himself, after his victory, 'I inherited; I bought; I conquered'.

The acquisition of Portugal was enormously significant for Spain. The addition of the Portuguese empire brought Philip substantial possessions in the Far East, India, Africa and Brazil. The combination of Portuguese access to the spices, silks and precious stones of the East Indies and Spain's sources of bullion in the Americas was a potent one. Lisbon's bankers, already closely associated with Spain through their loans to the Crown, could now access the gold and silver of the Indies trade more directly, and Lisbon provided an important deep-water port on the Atlantic coast. The Azores stood astride the routes to both Spain's and Portugal's overseas possessions, acting as a rendezvous point for the Indies fleets. The combined Spanish and Portuguese fleet was the largest on earth, totalling almost 300,000 tons, although it was fully extended defending the immense lines of communication to the colonies. Meanwhile, the negotiation of peace with the Turks meant that the Spanish Empire now became a Westward-facing entity, with an Atlantic focus and Atlantic interests. The era of the Mediterranean was passing, and the shifting focus of Philip's attention vividly exemplified this. Granvelle's advice of 1586 reflects the change of perspective at the Spanish court.

1 While France is devastated by civil war, and the Turk is seriously weak-
   ened by the attacks of Persia, the government will find it advantageous
   to transfer itself to Portugal, for there it can draw on the resources of
   the Mediterranean and the Atlantic in order to launch the attack on
5 England and continue the pacification of the Netherlands.[4]

5 Analysis: The High Point of Philippine Foreign Policy?

> **KEY ISSUE** How successful was Philip II's foreign policy in the
> first half of his reign (1556–1584)?

1583 was perhaps the high point of Philip's reign. The acquisition of Portugal brought him huge new sources of revenue and a bigger fleet. He was at peace with the Turks and still had not finally burnt his bridges with Elizabeth of England. Spain's great rival, France remained hamstrung by a chaotic civil war, and the Duke of Parma,

Alexander Farnese, had begun to roll back the Dutch rebels, welding the southern provinces of the Netherlands into a unified entity, through assiduous diplomacy and military skill. The bullion of the Indies was flooding into Spanish coffers in greater quantities than ever before, yielding two or three million ducats per year during the 1580s. Had Philip died in 1583, he would surely have been praised for the skill with which he had pursued such a glorious foreign policy.

However, this success masked a number of growing problems, which threatened to derail Philip's efforts to maintain and extend his possessions. The peace with England was very tenuous, and was increasingly threatened by the vexed issue of Mary Stuart, who remained Elizabeth's prisoner, although the English Queen clearly did not know what to do about her royal captive. More seriously, developments in the Indies and the Netherlands increasingly brought England and Spain into conflict with one another and called into question the capacity of the two monarchs to restrain the hotter heads around them who called for war. Even so, 1583 clearly does represent the high watermark of Philip's empire, and perhaps the very success that he was enjoying convinced Philip that God favoured his cause. Chapter 8 examines how, emboldened by his successes, and by the steady stream of bullion reaching his Treasury, Philip took the opportunity to go over onto the offensive, with disastrous results. Concessions to the Dutch rebels, which Parma urged the King to grant, were withheld, promises were made to Catholic conspirators in France that Spain would support their efforts to exclude Henry of Navarre from the throne and, most disastrous of all, Philip allowed himself to be drawn into a conflict with Elizabeth of England, something he had stoutly resisted for 25 years.

References

1   Adapted from G. Parker, 'Lepanto: The Costs of Victory' in *Spain and the Netherlands* (Collins, 1979), p. 130.
2   Cited in A. Stiles, *The Ottoman Empire* (Hodder, 1989), p. 102.
3   F. Braudel, *The Mediterranean in the Age of Philip II* (Collins, 1973), p. 1103.
4   Cited in J. Lynch, *Spain 1516–1598* (Oxford, 1991), p. 439.

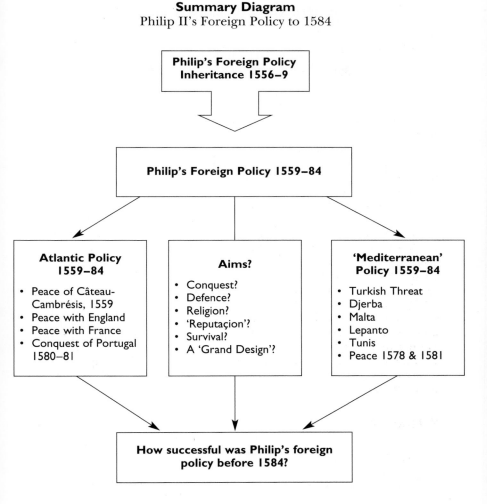

Summary Diagram
Philip II's Foreign Policy to 1584

Philip's Foreign Policy Inheritance 1556–9

Philip's Foreign Policy 1559–84

Atlantic Policy 1559–84

- Peace of Câteau-Cambrésis, 1559
- Peace with England
- Peace with France
- Conquest of Portugal 1580–81

Aims?

- Conquest?
- Defence?
- Religion?
- 'Reputaçion'?
- Survival?
- A 'Grand Design'?

'Mediterranean' Policy 1559–84

- Turkish Threat
- Djerba
- Malta
- Lepanto
- Tunis
- Peace 1578 & 1581

How successful was Philip's foreign policy before 1584?

Working on Chapter 7

The main theme of this chapter has been the degree to which Philip's handling of foreign policy before 1584 was successful. In your note making you should assess the success or failure of each theatre of foreign policy and then of foreign policy as a whole during this period. Foreign policy is a frequent theme of examination questions, so it is important that you get to grips with the factual detail and the issues. The Summary Diagram above can be used as a basis for a pattern approach to your note-making,

Answering structured questions on Chapter 7

Structured questions on this period of Philip's foreign policy might well take the following forms. The notes you have made on this chapter should enable you to answer them.

a) How strong was Spain internationally at the accession of Philip II?

b) Explain Philip II's success in absorbing Portugal into his empire between 1580–1583.

c) How successfully did Philip II preserve Spanish interests in the Mediterranean during the first half of his reign 1556-1581?

Question a) appears at first sight essentially descriptive, but a closer look reveals that it asks to you measure the strength of Spain, which requires evaluative judgement. Two 'lists', Causes of Strength and Causes of Weakness, will help you to address the issue clearly. Remember, the question asks for a snapshot picture of Spain at a certain point in time. Questions b) and c) are more evaluative. Question b) asks for an explanation of Philip's victory over Portugal. Remember to set the Portugal campaign against its international context, because this was significant. Philip had a rare period of breathing space during which to act decisively in Portugal, due to record proceeds from the bullion fleet, the truce with the Turks and the continued civil disorder within France. Finally, c) focuses on Spain's struggle with the Turks over control of the Mediterranean. It is tempting when faced with this sort of question to simply narrate the story of the conflict, focusing on the 'big events', Djerba, Malta and Lepanto. But this question is more evaluative than this and demands that you weigh up the successes and setbacks Philip experienced during the conflict before assessing whether he preserved Spanish 'interests'. You will have to decide what Spanish interests were, and the relative importance of various factors. Did Philip achieve his aims in the region by war or by peace, in the end?

Essay questions on Philip II's foreign policy will almost invariably require that you consider his reign in its entirety and consequently these will be addressed at the end of Chapter Eight.

Source-based questions on Chapter 7

1 The Victory at Lepanto

Study the table on page 99 and El Greco's painting on page 101. Then answer the questions that follow.

a) Study Table 1 on page 99. How far does this support the view that Lepanto was not the end of the Turkish threat in the Mediterranean? (3 marks)

b) How useful is El Greco's painting in describing the mood in Spain after the victory at Lepanto? *(4 marks)*

c) Compare Table 1 and El Greco's painting. How far do they differ regarding Spain's role in the victory? *(5 marks)*

d) Using both sources and your own knowledge, consider the view that the primary benefit derived from the victory at Lepanto was moral, not military. *(8 marks)*

8 Foreign Policy 1584–98

POINTS TO CONSIDER

The last 15 years of Philip II's reign brought a succession of foreign policy disasters. Spain faced a three-cornered challenge in the 1580s and 1590s from England, France and the rebel United Provinces of the Netherlands, who made common cause out of their shared fear and hatred of Spain, and their collaboration made it increasingly impossible for Philip to deal with a single problem in isolation. This chapter examines Philip's unavailing efforts to answer this challenge. Narrative notes on foreign policy can become long and complicated, so as you read this chapter for the first time, consider not only the major events but also the important issues driving Philip's foreign policy. Primarily, however, this chapter examines the causes, course and outcome of the wars that dominated Philip's declining years. What do they reveal about the pre-occupations and priorities of Philip's foreign policy in this period? Why were they so unproductive for Spain? How strong, internationally, did Philip leave his kingdom?

KEY DATES

1584 Treaty of Joinville between Philip II and the Catholic League in France.
1585 Treaty of Nonsuch between England and the Dutch rebels.
1587 Drake raids Cadiz.
1588 The Spanish Armada fails.
1589 Azores raid by English fleet fails.
1590 Spanish army relieves Henry IV's siege of Paris.
1595 Henry IV declares war on Spain.
1598 Treaty of Vervins ends the Franco-Spanish war.
1604 Treaty of London ends the war between Spain and England.

1 War with France

KEY ISSUES Why did Spain intervene in the French civil wars in the 1580s? What were the consequences of this intervention for Spanish foreign policy?

In 1584, Henry III's brother, Francis Duke of Anjou died, leaving their cousin Henry of Navarre, a Protestant, as the Heir Presumptive to the crown of France. The prospect of a Protestant occupying the French throne filled Philip with foreboding. Already enmeshed in the Dutch Revolt, Philip felt certain that a Protestant King of France would seek common cause with the Netherlands rebels. Philip also feared that Henry of Navarre would encourage the spread of heresy into northern Spain. Consequently, Philip decided to support more openly and directly the radical Catholic cause in France: 'It seems to be the only way to remedy matters of religion in that kingdom.'[1] On 31st December 1584 he signed the Treaty of Joinville with the noble leaders of the Catholic League, the Dukes of Guise and Mayenne, promising to subsidise their military operations, even if this meant fighting directly against the French crown. The treaty strongly favoured Spain. In return for Philip's assistance, the Catholic League promised to prevent the accession of Navarre, favouring instead Henry's uncle, the Roman Catholic Cardinal of Bourbon. In addition, the decrees of the Council of Trent (see pages 65–6), hitherto unenforced in France would become 'fundamental laws' of France, the French alliance with the Turks would be ended and French privateering against Spain's Atlantic shipping would end.

However, Philip found himself drawn into deeper and deeper involvement in the French civil war. In January 1589, Henry III was murdered and Navarre became Henry IV. Philip's nightmare scenario of a Protestant succession in France appeared to be coming true. Philip resolved to exclude Henry of Navarre from the throne by force if necessary, and ordered the Duke of Parma, commanding the Army of Flanders, to intervene. Why did Philip allow himself to be so drawn into France's affairs? He seems to have been motivated by a combination of fear for Spanish security and religious zeal, although the latter consideration dominated his instructions to his subordinates. Writing to the Duke of Parma in the Netherlands, he argued:

1 My principal aim is to secure the well-being of the Faith, and to see that in France Catholicism survives and heresy is excluded ... If, in order to ensure this ... it is necessary for my troops to enter France openly ... it seems that we must do something about the war in the Netherlands,
5 reducing it to a defensive footing.[2]

Later, his other concern, for security, was outlined: 'If the heretics were to prevail (which I hope that God will not allow) it might open the door to worse damage and dangers and to war at home.'[3]

Parma objected strongly that he was on the verge of success against the Dutch rebels, and that the diversion would allow his enemies to regroup. Although others at Court echoed his doubts, Philip overruled the doubters, writing to Mateo Vazquez in January 1591 that 'the cause of religion must take precedence over everything'.[4] The outcome of this more aggressive interventionism on Philip's part was war between Spain and France. In 1590, Parma led the Army of Flanders into France to support the League against Henry IV. Parma was successful in relieving the siege of Paris, and in April 1592, a second campaign relieved the siege of Rouen. However, Parma's fears proved correct. The Dutch took advantage of his absence to refortify their defences and reorganise their army, and his refusal to lead a third intervention in France's internal struggles in 1593 resulted in his dismissal.

Ironically, Philip's intervention worsened the situation of the League, as Henry IV's propagandists identified their enemies with Spain and foreign invasion, portraying them as traitors. During 1592 and 1593, Philip's ambassador in Paris tried to persuade the Estates General (France's 'parliament') to set aside the Salic Law of Inheritance (which stipulated that no King of France could inherit the throne through the female line of succession), and to proclaim Philip's daughter by Elisabeth de Valois, Isabella, Queen of France, possibly as consort of the young Duke of Guise. These efforts only alienated many Frenchmen, and Henry IV chose this moment to announce his conversion to Catholicism, an act that robbed the Catholic League of their principal argument against him, his religion. By 1595, the Catholic cause was as good as lost. In January 1595, Henry IV, whose conversion had, by now, been ratified by the Pope himself, declared war on Spain, calling upon all Frenchmen to assist him in expelling the Spanish 'invader'. After a series of brilliant French victories in Burgundy and Normandy, the Leaguer nobles sued for peace. To make matters worse, in 1596, England, France and the United Provinces formed the Triple Alliance, an explicitly anti-Spanish treaty. Spain found herself bereft of allies and enmeshed in a war she had not expected against a united France. At this point bankruptcy forced Philip to seek a truce. The Treaty of Vervins, signed in 1598, ended the war inconclusively, with the terms of Câteau-Cambrésis reconfirmed.

Philip's intervention in France was possibly the most indefensible and catastrophic decision of his reign. Already over-committed elsewhere, Philip allowed his heart to rule his head, placing religious considerations and his fears of a hostile Protestant French neighbour above his pressing need for a manageable and affordable foreign policy. He failed to appreciate that any Spanish intervention in French affairs would only unite all French men against Philip's allies, and that no Protestant would be able to accede to the throne of an overwhelmingly Catholic nation such as France without significant difficulties. Henry IV would almost certainly have converted to Catholicism without Philip's pressure, and all that Philip achieved was the further alienation of France and the dissipation of Spain's already dwindling resources in yet another conflict. Intervention in France merely ensured that Spain's enemies united against her, for there was little else to bind together England, France and the Netherlands rebels except fear of Spain.

2 The 'Enterprise on England'

> **KEY ISSUES** Why did Spain launch the Spanish Armada? Why did it fail?

a) Why did Philip launch the 'Enterprise on England'?

In August 1585 Elizabeth I of England concluded the Treaty of Nonsuch with the Dutch rebels, under which Elizabeth agreed to aid their struggle against Spain by sending £126,000 and 6,000 troops, commanded by the Earl of Leicester, to the Netherlands, in return for the 'cautionary towns' of Flushing, Brill and Rammekens. The treaty was the culmination of a gradual deterioration of Anglo-Spanish relations during the previous 15 years over the Indies, Elizabeth's imprisonment of Mary Stuart and English support for the Dutch Revolt (see Chapter 7). Moreover, Philip had been under pressure for years, from the Papacy, from his ambassadors in London and from his more adventurous commanders, to invade England and overthrow England's Protestant regime. Although he had skilfully diverted such demands before 1585, the pressure became impossible to resist following Elizabeth's intervention in the Netherlands. In short, although Elizabeth may have regarded the Treaty of Nonsuch as a diplomatic move, intended to put pressure on Spain to open peace negotiations with the rebels, the English intervention was regarded in Spain as an act of war, a view reinforced when Sir Francis Drake, with a small flotilla, raided the Spanish coastline in October 1585.

The conflict that followed is most famed for the Spanish Armada, but it dragged on for nearly twenty years, only ending, inconclusively, in 1604. Ironically, the 6,000 English troops sent to the Netherlands were ineffective. Indeed, in 1589, English troops garrisoning St Gertruidenburg surrendered it to Parma in return for the payment of arrears of wages. The real fighting was confined to a series of inconclusive naval campaigns. From the outset the centrepiece of Philip's strategy was the 'Enterprise on England'. In 1585, he demanded that his senior commanders, Santa Cruz and Parma, draw up plans for such an enterprise. To what purpose? Although some historians regard the Armada expedition as an expensive warning, designed to cow the English into surrender and discourage English interference in Spain's affairs, others argue that the intent was to invade and militarily defeat England, forcing her, at the very least, to allow the practice of Catholicism again. The rhetoric of the King and his senior commanders seems to support the latter view. The Jesuit, Ribadeneyra, wrote in an exhortation to the troops:

> I consider this enterprise the most important undertaken by God's Church for many hundreds of years. Every conceivable pretext for a just and holy war is to be found in this campaign ... this is a

defensive, not an offensive war; one in which we are defending our
5 sacred religion and our most holy Roman Catholic faith; one in
which we are defending the high reputation of our King and lord,
and of our nation too; defending, too, the land and property of all
the kingdoms of Spain, and simultaneously our peace, tranquillity and
repose.[5]

Whilst the ships and stockpiles of supplies for the 'Enterprise on
England' assembled in a group of western ports, orders went out to
Parma in the Netherlands to ready his forces for transportation over
to England as part of a huge amphibious invasion. Parma was unim-
pressed, both with the plans Philip forwarded to him, and with the
total failure to keep the project secret. A measure of this failure came
in April 1587, when Drake brilliantly raided Cadiz, burning several
ships and destroying supplies, and thereby delaying the Armada's
departure. A further setback occurred when Santa Cruz, the commander of the entire operation, died in February 1588. His replacement, the Duke of Medina Sidonia, although no sailor, was an
experienced land commander and a talented and energetic adminis-
trator and the Armada, already several months behind schedule,
needed his organisational skills.

b) Why did the Armada fail?

Finally, in May 1588, the Spanish Armada set sail. After a month's
delay at La Coruña, following a sudden storm, the fleet recommenced
their journey northwards in July, only to be outmanoeuvred in the
Channel and destroyed by foul weather in the North Sea. Why was it
such a disaster? Contemporaries and historians have picked over the
campaign in enormous detail, searching for an explanation, but the
reasons were manifold. Firstly, the plan chosen (from several available) by Philip was excessively complicated. It called for a fleet of war-
ships and supply ships to sail from Lisbon to Dunkirk, where it would
link up with a fleet of barges carrying Parma's invasion force. They
would then sail across the Channel to Kent, land somewhere near
Margate and advance directly to London. This plan combined the
worst features of two original proposals, invasion directly from Spain
(Santa Cruz's plan) and an unescorted surprise attack by Parma's
army from Dunkirk (Parma's plan). Crucially there was no provision
for the close co-ordination of the two fleets. How was Parma to know
precisely when to be embarked and ready? This would prove a fatal
weakness.

Secondly, the Spanish fleet was outgunned by their English enemies, which enabled the English to prevent the juncture of the two
forces. Oddly enough, the Spanish were aware of this problem before
even setting sail. In a dispatch to Medina Sidonia in April 1588 Philip
noted:

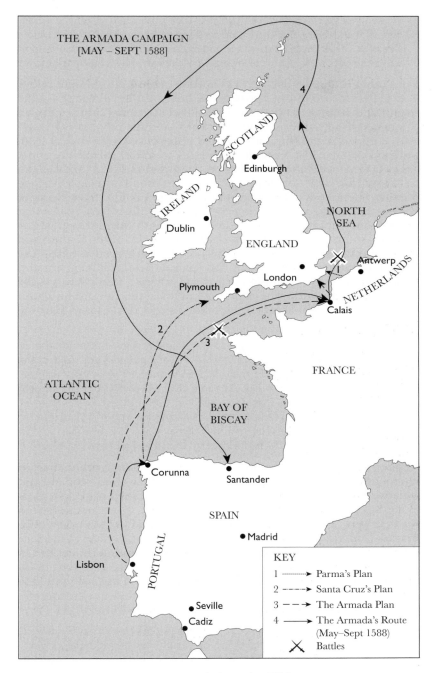

The Spanish Armada, 1588

> The enemy's objective will be to fight at long distance, to get the advantage of his artillery and shot (said to be in great quantity) ... The objective of our fleet must be to attack and close with them, ready for hand to hand combat ... He should also be told of the way they have of firing low.[6]

Yet although the Spanish fleet, as a whole, consisted of large, rather slow galleons, and did not possess the heavy artillery throughout the fleet that the English did, there were sufficient capital ships equipped to engage the English in a straight fight. Medina Sidonia was, however, no naval tactician, and his rigid adherence to his orders from Philip prevented him from deploying his resources effectively in the series of encounters between the two fleets as they sailed up the channel in August 1588. Anchoring off Calais in the first week of August, Medina Sidonia waited for Parma's barges to emerge from Dunkirk before continuing on, ignoring the protests of his subordinates that Parma could not leave Dunkirk unescorted with fully loaded barges, otherwise his troop carriers would be sitting ducks for the English and Dutch ships anchored outside. Whilst the fleet dithered at Calais, the English sent in fireships, forcing the Spanish fleet to slip anchor and scatter out into the Channel once more, where a fierce naval battle ensued off Gravelines. The superior English guns and gunnery won the day and the Armada fled, before a rapidly rising wind, into the North Sea.

> We found the enemy with a great advantage in ships, better than ours for battle, better designed, with better artillery, gunners and sailors, and so rigged they could handle them and do with them what they wanted. The strength of our Armada was some twenty vessels, and they fought
> 5 very well, better even than they needed, but the rest fled whenever they saw the enemy attack. Of that I will say nothing in my account to save the reputation of our nation. Furthermore, we brought so few cannon balls that I hardly had a fighting ship that had anything to fire.[7]

As the storm rose, the Spanish ships had no choice other than to attempt to return to Spain via a dangerous route around Scotland and Ireland. A month later the 60 surviving ships limped back into ports along Spain's northern coast. More damagingly, 15,000 experienced seamen were lost, including several senior naval commanders. The Armada's surviving commanders returned in disgrace. Parma lost face with Philip and his enemies at court were able to undermine him in the years that followed, and Medina Sidonia was taunted in the streets. Afterwards, a medal was minted in England and the Netherlands, carrying the legend 'God blew and they were scattered', and the historian Fernandez-Armesto agrees with this analysis:

> The most widespread contemporary analysis of the Armada's failure, attributing it to winds — whether of natural or providential origin — seems justified. Most of the reasons adduced by historians can be admitted in varying degrees but only in an ancillary role. It may well be true,

5 for instance, that the Armada was foredoomed to failure from the start
   by errors of strategic planning and co-ordination; but ... English strategy was equally deficient ... Similarly, though Spanish tactics were
   unworkable, those of the English were ineffective. Differences in tactics
   made only a marginal difference to the course, and can only have made
10 a marginal difference to the outcome, of the Armada fights ... Every
   conceivable kind of technical deficiency has been invoked in explanation
   of the Armada's failure. Deficiencies in the build of Spanish ships ...
   were real enough to make Spanish victory unlikely, but ... in only a few
   cases were weak build and bad design primarily responsible for ship
15 losses – and even here, only to the weather ... English superiority in the
   overall fighting strength of their fleet, ordnance, quality of shot, design
   of gun carriages and expertise in gunnery made some contribution, but
   not enough to disable more than three Spanish ships. The myth of generally inferior Spanish seamanship has to be dismissed altogether.[8]

The financial cost, 10 million ducats, was crippling and could only be
met by the levy of a new tax, the *millones*. Rather surprisingly, the normally querulous Cortes was supportive: 'Everything possible must be
done... to defeat (the English), to repair the recent loss and to
restore the reputation of our nation'.[9] But the damage extended far
beyond the war with England. The diversion of Parma's forces from
their hitherto successful campaigns in Netherlands gave the rebels
breathing space in which to strengthen the defences and reorganise.
Moreover, the immense cost of the armada drew funds from Parma's
army. After a ten-year period during which the army of Flanders had
been properly paid and supplied, mutiny broke out again in 1589.
Twenty more mutinies would follow in the next decade. Although
new fleets were built and Philip's determination to defeat Elizabeth
was unshaken, the failure of the Armada was indeed the beginning of
the end of Spain's 'Golden Age'.

3 The Anglo-Spanish War

> **KEY ISSUE** What were the consequences for Spain of the long
> war against England?

The defeat of the Armada was not, as English tradition often suggests,
the end of the Spanish threat. Rather, it was the beginning of a long
and unproductive conflict, from which neither side profited. Philip II
told his council, in November 1588, that:

1 I was moved to undertake the Armada campaign for the service of Our
   Lord, the defence of His Cause, and the advantage of these realms ... I
   still feel the same now, and greatly desire that our efforts should
   achieve what has become all the more necessary because of what has
5 happened.[10]

In the years that followed, a second and third armada (in 1596 and 1597) was assembled, but neither reached its destination, due once again to adverse weather. Around 400 Spanish troops did land briefly in Cornwall in 1595, burning Penzance before being driven off.[11] However, whilst the merest threat of another armada was enough to strike panic into English hearts, the enormous cost of these expeditions placed an intolerable burden upon Spain's finances. English naval expeditions were barely more successful. Drake raided the coastline of northern Spain in 1589, but a raid on the Azores in 1591 was driven off with heavy losses by the rebuilt Spanish navy, and a further landing in Portugal made little impact. Repeated English raids in the Indies met with only partial success. The Holy Grail of such expeditions, the capture of the bullion fleet, was never achieved and on the 1595 expedition to Panama, Drake died. However, in July 1596 the Earl of Essex succeeded in capturing and holding Cadiz for a fortnight. The city was pillaged relentlessly, much to Philip's embarrassment, and before sailing away (unmolested) the English set the city alight. The whole episode was regarded as a national humiliation by Spaniards.

Throughout the 1590s, the struggle continued on land in the Netherlands, where England aided the Dutch rebels, and France, particularly Brittany and Normandy, where both English and Spanish forces intervened in France's internal conflicts. Meanwhile, Philip attempted to stir up Elizabeth's Irish subjects, led by the rebellious Earl of Tyrone. Tyrone's rebellion between 1597 and 1599 tied down 17,000 English troops, and 4,500 Spanish troops landed in Ireland in 1601, although they made little impression and were eventually forced to surrender at Kinsale. But whereas Philip needed to defeat Elizabeth, the English required merely that Spain remained tied down in multiple theatres of warfare until her finances collapsed. In this respect, it might be argued that England 'won' the fitful and inconclusive exchanges of the Anglo-Spanish War, although the damage done to the important trading relationships that had existed between the two countries was enduring, and reinforces the impression of a war that neither side really 'won'. The Treaty of London finally brought peace in 1604, but hostilities had effectively petered-out several years previously.

4 The Debate over Philip's Foreign Policy

> **KEY ISSUE** What were the aims and objectives of Philip II's foreign policy?

Philip's foreign policy was controversial even during his own lifetime. Philip's enemies argued that Spain was aggressive and expansionist, and that he sought to establish 'Universal Monarchy'.

Contemporaries, especially in Protestant Europe, interpreted Philip's ill-considered attempt to place his daughter on the French and English thrones as a plan for Habsburg hegemony over Europe. Henry of Navarre's propagandists claimed that Philip sought 'to make himself absolute lord of all France'.[12] Such ideas gained apparent support from the medal struck in 1583 to mark Spain's acquisition of Portugal's empire, which proclaimed 'The world is not enough'. Even Philip's allies were alive to the possibility. The Pope, in a letter to his ambassador in Paris in 1589, suggested that Philip's motives were primarily self-interested:

> The King of Spain, as a temporal sovereign, is anxious above all to safeguard and increase his dominions ... The preservation of the Catholic religion ... is only a pretext for His Majesty, whose principal aim is the security and aggrandisement of his dominions.[13]

Some historians have agreed that Philip had expansionist goals. R Trevor Davies argued, in 1937:

1 To Philip, no doubt, all his policy was consciously directed to the glory of God and the good of His Church; but these things were identical in his mind with the exaltation of the power of Spain ... Whenever political interest and religious zeal clashed, religious zeal almost invariably
5 gave way.[14]

Generally, the 'Universal Monarchy' theory should be seen for the sixteenth Century 'Black Legend' propaganda that it was. However, in Protestant Europe, Spanish foreign policy was suspected of serving the Catholic cause. Elizabeth I's spymaster Sir Francis Walsingham argued that an international Catholic conspiracy, with its centre in Rome and Madrid, was working to exterminate Protestantism. This thesis was repeated in Amsterdam and Geneva, where Spain was perceived as the principal threat to European Protestantism. How valid was this view? Did Philip seek to become the 'Champion of Christendom'? Certainly, the defence of Catholicism was a traditional foreign policy priority of the Spanish monarchs, and Philip was a devout Catholic. The nineteenth century German historian von Ranke argued that religion was the driving force of Philip's foreign policy, and other, more recent historians have taken up this theme:

1 His prior and unquestioning task was to defend in arms the interests of God and His Church ... It was the essence of the contract between the Habsburg rulers and their maker and benefactor, that they would unceasingly advance His cause, just as He automatically protected
5 theirs.[15]

Certainly one motivation for the Armada against England in 1588 was religious. Medina Sidonia's orders to the fleet before they set sail for England stated:

1 The principal reason which has moved his Majesty to undertake this
   enterprise is his desire to serve God, and to convert to His Church
   many peoples and souls who are now oppressed by the heretical enemies of our holy Catholic faith, and are subjected to their sects and
5 errors.[16]

However, whilst religion undoubtedly influenced Philip's thinking, it
seems unlikely that religious objectives predominated in the shaping
of policy. Although Philip spent the first 20 years of his reign at war
with the Turks, there were excellent strategic and defensive reasons
for this, irrespective of religious considerations. Equally, it is true that
Philip's attitude to Protestant heretics, famously expressed in his
claim in 1566 that 'rather than suffer the slightest prejudice to
religion I would prefer to lose all my dominions and a hundred lives
if I had them', was hostile. But words are cheap, and if the proof of
his ardour is sought in action, the evidence is inconclusive. Malta and
Lepanto represented important Christian victories over the Turks,
but Philip's readiness to make peace with the Sultan in 1581 suggests
a more ambiguous attitude, and his invasion in 1580 of Portugal, a
fellow Catholic country, seems to scotch the idea that his policies were
motivated by religious considerations. Towards the end of his life, religious considerations may have assumed greater centrality in his thinking. Ministers protesting against Spain's military intervention in
France were told 'These are not matters which can be dropped...
because they involve the cause of religion, which must take precedence over everything'.[17]

The Venetian Ambassador offered a more cautious contemporary
analysis of Philip's motives:

1 His Majesty has been aiming not to wage war, so that he can add to his
   kingdoms but to wage peace, so that he can keep the lands that he has
   .... If he wanted to imitate the Emperor ... his enormous resources
   combined with some luck would make him feared throughout the
5 world ... But he differs from him in many of the respects that make
   rulers truly great. His father loved the battleground and mastered the
   arts of war, but his son dislikes warfare and knows little about it. The
   Emperor undertook great campaigns of conquest, but the King avoids
   them. Charles planned great projects and eventually carried them
10 through with enormous profit to himself, but Philip cares less about his
   own grandeur than he does about blocking the progress of others.[18]

This seems to suggest that Philip was primarily motivated by the
defence of his dynastic inheritance, seeking only to protect the
Netherlands, the Western Mediterranean, and Spanish possessions
elsewhere against foreign threat, and to pass on his inheritance intact
to his son. Indeed Philip consistently argued that 'I have no intention
of breaking the general peace, which is a thing I myself most wish to
preserve', claiming 'God is my witness that I have never made war to
gain more kingdoms, but only to maintain them in the faith and in

peace'. Whilst this appears to be contradicted by the invasion of Portugal, it should be stressed that Philip could reasonably claim to be protecting his rightful inheritance when he invaded Portugal in 1580.

Other historians have argued that personal honour and Spanish pride were key considerations. In the sixteenth century, the foreign policy of a nation often served the honour and '*reputaçion*' of the monarch more than the interests of the nation. Woodward suggests that 'honour and reputation meant more to Philip than the acquisition of new lands, fighting religious wars, or the creation of a universal monarchy',[19] and certainly Philip was acutely conscious of his '*reputaçion*', arguing in 1557 that his war against France was in defence of 'my states, as well as my honour and *reputaçion*, which I value above all else'.[20] However, he did not wage war for this reason alone, although it may have provided an element of his thinking at crucial moments. During the Netherlands revolt, Philip refused to grant concessions to the rebels because to do so would be dishonourable, even if this meant the continuation of a ruinous war. However, surely more weighty was the argument that to make an ignominious peace was to signal to his other enemies and to potentially rebellious subjects that he (and, by implication, Spain) was weak. As one minister observed in 1566: 'If the Netherlands situation is not remedied it will bring about the loss of Spain and all the rest'.

In his defence, Philip rarely had the luxury to devise a policy and pursue it. His foreign policy can be viewed as little more than a series of short-term responses to individual crises, but this is only a partial explanation. Philip, like other early modern rulers, possessed limited bureaucratic and technological means, and often devised and pursued policy within circumscribed limits, hemmed in by events and developments, as he saw it, outside his control. But equally his response to events was shaped, to some extent, by a 'world view', an ideological or strategic framework. Parker has recently revived the idea that Philip did possess a 'Grand Design' for his '*monarquia*'.[21] Although this was not necessarily a blueprint for empire, as his enemies asserted, it did lead him to commit acts of aggression towards his neighbours, driven above all by his perception of himself as God's instrument for the defence and furtherance of the Catholic faith. It is striking how frequently Philip claimed that a given project would succeed because God would ensure that it did. He wrote to Requesens in the Netherlands that 'You are engaged in God's service and in mine, which is the same thing'. Such 'providentialism' was hardly unusual in early modern Europe (Cromwell was famous for his faith in Providence, as were most Calvinists), but Parker perhaps overstates the messianic nature of Philip's self-perception as 'God's servant'.

Philip II's foreign policy objectives remain controversial, and an accurate assessment of his motives probably lies in a combination of factors, the precise mix of which varied according to circumstance and the perspective from which one views the question. The late sixteenth century was an era of imperial conflict, in which Philip's enemies, viewing his policies from Amsterdam, Paris and London, could plausibly regard Spain as aggressive and expansionist. The annexation of Portugal, the appearance of Spanish troops in Paris during the 1590s and the armadas sent against England provided evidence supporting this view. However, modern research shows us a monarch struggling to preserve his widely scattered and vulnerable monarchy against a sea of enemies. Philip's wars were usually, in his mind, defensive, fought primarily to protect his inheritance and defend his and Spain's interests. Spain did not seek to annex territories that did not legitimately belong to her. Even in the invasion of Portugal in 1580 Philip had arguably the strongest claim of any candidate to the throne. Philip always claimed that he acted within his rights as King of Spain and that he sought only to defend his inheritance, his faith and Spain's interests. However, he failed to appreciate that the robust defence, by force of arms if necessary, of his legitimate interests, appeared proof of hostile intent and was consequently viewed with alarm by his neighbours. This difference of perspective offers a possible explanation for the different interpretations of Philippine foreign policy.

5 Conclusion – Success or Failure?

> **KEY ISSUES** How successful was Philip II's foreign policy? How strong was Spain at the time of Philip II's death?

It is arguable whether Philip II's foreign policy promoted the interests of Spain or of the Habsburg dynasty, but to an extent this would be an artificial distinction to make, since in the sixteenth century there was no modern concept of the national interest and the two would have been regarded as inseparable. Philip II **was** Spain, and his interests were hers. A more pressing issue is whether Philip's foreign policy achieved its objectives although, inevitably, our answer to this question is partially determined by our view of precisely what Philip sought to achieve. Equally, when considering Philip's foreign policy the inter-relationship between foreign policy and imperial policy (especially in the Netherlands and the Indies) is vital. English piracy on the 'Spanish Main' and intervention in the Dutch Revolt ultimately poisoned Philip's initially cordial relations with Elizabeth of England, and the connections between Dutch and French Protestantism played a part in dragging Philip into France's civil war.

Seen from 1598, Philip's foreign policy appears disastrous. At his death, Spain was bankrupt, embroiled in an expensive but unproductive war with England and no nearer than in 1572 to ending the rebellion in the Netherlands. Indeed, Philip's decision to grant his

daughter Isabella and her husband Albert of Austria the archduke-
dom of the 'Spanish Netherlands' appeared to recognise the loss of
the northern provinces, although the conflict dragged on for a further decade. Worse, in many contemporaries' eyes, was the loss of
'*reputaçion*' as a result of the Armada defeat and the defeat by France.
Insiders in Philip's government believed that Spain had taken on too
many commitments and had failed to undertake decisive action in
any one field, thus perpetuating a number of parallel conflicts, which
bled the human and financial resources of the country, and made victory in any one conflict unattainable. Padilla argued that 'wars thus
become chronic, and the expense and trouble resulting from long
continued wars are endless'.[22]

Philip's failure to avoid new commitments or cut his losses in one
theatre so as better to concentrate them elsewhere was crucial to the
ultimate collapse of all his projects. He constantly restated that to
concede defeat in one area would be to invite challenge elsewhere,
and he was most reluctant to cede possession of lands inherited from
his father. This was particularly so in the Netherlands, where Philip
refused to compromise or admit defeat for 30 years, expending thousands of lives and perhaps 80 million ducats to retain control over his
father's ancestral lands. This consciousness of his dynastic duty
expressed itself in a sort of 'domino theory', preventing him from
making a realistic assessment of the regime's capacity to defend and
maintain its possessions.

In the early part of his reign Philip by and large pursued limited,
defensive policies. Even this entailed multiple commitments in the
Netherlands and the Mediterranean, leading to a state bankruptcy in
1575. Nevertheless, by 1580 he had maintained peace with France
and England, had stemmed the Turkish tide and had successfully
invaded and conquered Portugal. Even in the Netherlands, things
were beginning to improve. From the perspective of 1580, Philip's
management of foreign policy appears shrewd and successful. After
this date, however, the tone of Philip's policy became more aggressive. Legitimate or not, Philip's acquisition of the crown of Portugal in
1580 alarmed other European powers, but he failed to appreciate
how threatened his other neighbours felt by the further expansion of
the already immense Spanish empire. His adoption of an aggressive
policy towards England (albeit with some justification, given the
provocation endured at English hands in the preceding years) and his
intervention in France significantly raised the stakes in Europe. Yet to
the end Philip did not regard himself as an aggressor. Why was he
unable to see what the rest of Europe saw so plainly? The explanation
may be sought in the rhetoric with which he urged his subordinates
on during the last two decades of his life. His correspondence with
ministers and commanders was increasingly dominated by a belief
that he was engaged upon God's work and that he could not fail
because God would bless his endeavours, however ill conceived and

hare-brained! His policies in France show him increasingly inclined to place his religious duty to defend the Catholic faith above other considerations. Towards the end of his life, then, Philip's ideological rigidity led him to take on commitments that good sense would have counselled against. The outcome of this was to over-commit Spain and thereby to hamstring her efforts in each and every theatre of war, leading eventually to multiple defeats and financial and economic ruin.

References

1 Cited in G. Woodward, *Philip II* (Longman, 1992), p. 76.
2 Cited in G. Parker, *The Grand Strategy of Philip II* (Yale, 1998), p. 273.
3 Cited in *Ibid.*, p. 275.
4 Cited in *Ibid.*, p. 276.
5 Cited in J. H. Elliott, *Imperial Spain* (Penguin, 1963), p. 288.
6 Cited in G. Parker, 'Why the Armada Failed' in *History Today* (May 1988), p. 33.
7 Don Francisco de Bobadilla, cited in J. Lotherington ed., *Years of Renewal* (Hodder, 1999), p. 455.
8 F. Fernandez-Armesto, *The Spanish Armada* (Oxford, 1989) p. 268.
9 Cited in Parker, *The Grand Strategy of Philip II*, p. 271.
10 Cited in C. Martin & G. Parker, *The Spanish Armada* (Mandolin, Manchester, 1999), p. 245.
11 See G. Darby, 'The Spanish Armada of ... 1597?' in *The Historian* 55 (1997), p. 14.
12 Anon, 'An Admonition to the Duke of Savoy' (1589), cited in J. Lock, 'How Many Tercios has the Pope? The Spanish War and the Sublimation of Elizabethan Anti-Popery' in *History* 81 (1996), p. 207.
13 Instructions from Pope Sixtus V to Cardinal Caetini, Papal ambassador in France, 1589. Cited in J. Lynch, 'Philip II and the Papacy', in *Transactions of the Royal Historical Society* (1961), p. 23.
14 R. Trevor Davies, *The Golden Century of Spain, 1501–1621* (Macmillan, 1937), p. 131.
15 R. H. Stradling, *Europe and the Decline of Spain* (London, 1981), p. 27.
16 Cited in Martin & Parker, *The Spanish Armada*, p. 26.
17 Letter to Mateo Vazquez in 1591, cited in Parker, *The Grand Strategy of Philip II*, p. 93.
18 Ambassador Suriano, cited in J. C. Davis, *The Pursuit of Power* (Harper, New York, 1970), p. 69.
19 See G. Woodward, 'Philip II's Foreign Policy', in *History Review* 21, p. 9.
20 Letter to Juana, cited in M. J. Rodriguez Salgado, *The Changing Face of Empire* (Cambridge, 1988), pp. 169–170.
21 See Parker *The Grand Strategy of Philip II*.
22 Cited in *Ibid.*, p. 282.

Summary Diagram

PHILIP'S FOREIGN POLICY AFTER 1584	
War Against France	War Against England
• Supports Holy League against King • Treaty of Joinville, 1584 • Parma's intervention in France 1590, 1592 • Franco-Spanish War 1595–8 • Treaty of Vervins, 1598	• Treaty of Nonsuch, 1585 • Drake raids Cadiz, 1587 • Spanish Armada, 1558 • English raid on Azores, 1590 • Spain supports Irish rebellion against England

EVALUATING PHILIP II'S FOREIGN POLICY, 1556–98	
1. AIMS	
• A 'Universal Monarchy'? • The 'Champion of Catholicism'? • Defence of his inheritance?	• 'Reputaçion'? • 'A Grand Design'? • Was there a 'policy' at all?
2. ACHIEVEMENTS, SUCCESS OR FAILURE?	
Successes	Failures

• Held back the Turkish threat in the Mediterranean
    • Malta
    • Lepanto
• Neutralised England and France for much of the reign
• Conquered Portugal (1580)
• May have helped persuade Henry IV of France to become a Catholic
	• Could not prevent Turkish capture of Cyprus (1571) and Tunis (1574)
	• Anglo-Spanish war was disastrous
	    • Armada failed
	    • Cadiz raided in 1587 and 1596
	• Cost of incessant war bankrupted Spain (e.g. 1575, 1596)
	• Diverted Spain's efforts away from pacification of Netherlands Consequently lost northern provinces

Working on Chapter 8

This chapter has addressed a number of important issues and your notes need to be careful and detailed. Start by making brief narrative notes on the theatres of foreign policy examined in this chapter, France and England. These should connect with the notes you have on these areas from Chapter 7. Your notes on Philip's aims and objectives in foreign policy should enable you to offer examples of his objectives in action, if possible. List the main theories and see if you can identify moments when Philip's actions conform to this theory. A diagrammatical approach to this would perhaps work best. Finally, you will need to make analytical notes on the question of the success or failure of Philip's foreign policy by 1598. This might best be achieved by creating two shorter sets of notes, entitled SUCCESSES and FAILURES. Once you have listed these, look at the argument that Philip's foreign policy was successful before 1585 (see Chapter 7) but disastrous after that date. Write a brief (100 word) conclusion answering this question.

Answering essay questions on Chapter 8

Questions on Philip II's foreign policy tend to take three forms. Most will ask you to consider either the aims of his foreign policy or its effectiveness. Questions about the aims of Spanish foreign policy invite you to demonstrate your knowledge of the historical debate surrounding Philippine foreign policy. Question 1 below, a good example of the 'challenging statement' type of question, offers one possible explanation of the motives of Philippine foreign policy, and invites you to discuss this critically.

1. How far can Philip II's foreign policy be described as an attempt to defend the Catholic faith against Protestant and Muslim forces?

You are, of course, not expected simply to agree with the statement. Rather, you should weigh up the relative significance of religious considerations in Philip's foreign policy thinking alongside other factors. It is a useful rule of thumb to start your survey of the evidence with the theory that you have been offered in the question, in this case the argument that Philip was motivated primarily by religious factors. You will need to outline the argument that Philip was driven by his faith to undertake certain policies, perhaps considering the recent updating of the religion argument by Parker to stress the messianic elements of Philip's thinking. You then need to test these ideas against the evidence. Examine the main theatres and events in Philip's foreign policy and assess whether religion was the key issue at stake in each case. If, at the end of this, religion does not seem a sufficient explanation then you need to outline the arguments that you think explain Philippine policy more accurately. In your conclusion, you should indicate which view you agree with and why.

The evaluation of the success or failure of Philippine foreign policy is the other main theme that foreign policy questions tend to explore. Questions about the effectiveness of Philip's foreign policy can take various forms.

2. Consider the view that, on balance, the foreign policy of Philip II was successful in defending the interests of Spain.
3. Did the foreign policy of Philip II strengthen or weaken Spain?

However, you may be asked to evaluate the foreign policy of Spain in a broader sense. These sorts of questions call for an overview of the whole of Philip's foreign policy and require a balanced and selective approach.

4. How consistent was the foreign policy of Philip II in its aims and implementation?
5. How far is it possible to defend the foreign policy of Philip II?

Source-based questions on Chapter 8

1 Philip's Foreign Policy Aims
Study the extracts from R Trevor Davies on page 123, R. A. Stradling on page 123, Medina Sidonia on page 124 and the Venetian ambassador, Suriano on page 124. Then answer the questions that follow.

a) Who are the 'heretical enemies of our holy Catholic faith' referred to by Medina Sidonia (page 124, lines 3–4)? *(2 marks)*
b) In what ways does Suriano critically compare Philip II with his father, Charles? *(3 marks)*
c) Compare the judgements of the historians, Trevor Davies and Stradling, with the speech by Medina Sidonia. Which historian's viewpoint is supported by Medina Sidonia's evidence? *(5 marks)*
d) Using all the sources and your own knowledge, evaluate the view that Philip II's foreign policy was motivated primarily by a desire to protect his inheritance. *(10 marks)*

Many document questions require you to make a comparison between sources. In answering c) above, try to avoid just rehearsing the content of the three sources. This is a very low level response. Instead, try to pick out the key features of the single source (in this case, Medina Sidonia's speech), and then look for points to compare and contrast with this in the other two extracts. This way you should be able to provide examples of similarities and differences, and you should be able to draw a conclusion about which of the extracts Medina Sidonia's speech supports.

9 The Philippine Era – A Golden Age?

POINTS TO CONSIDER

This chapter primarily examines the legacy left behind by Philip II and some of the responses to his reign by contemporaries at the time of his death. It opens by considering whether Spain went through a decade of social, economic and political crisis during the 1590s, before exploring the cultural achievements of Spain during the reign of Philip II. Although some historians have argued that Spain retreated into an inward-looking cocoon during this period, there were many outstanding aesthetic achievements in Philippine Spain, mostly encouraged by the artistic patronage of the King himself. Is this significant? What does the art of a country or a period reveal about the nature of that society and era?

KEY DATES

1585	War breaks out between England and Spain.
1588–1591	Plague affects Valencia, Catalonia, Galicia and Murcia.
1590	Spanish armies intervene in the French civil wars.
	Protests against the *millones* occur in Madrid and other Castilian towns.
	France declares war on Spain.
1596	Philip declares bankruptcy for the third time.
1597	Plague strikes in Santander.
1598	Plague strikes in Madrid.
	Treaty of Vervins ends the war between France and Spain.
	Philip II dies. State debt stands at 87 million ducats.

1 The 'Crisis of the 1590s'

> **KEY ISSUE** Did Spain experience a decade of crisis in the 1590s?

In the last decade of Philip's life many of his projects fell to ruin. Famine and plague stalked Spain, the economy collapsed, the monarchy was assailed on all sides by enemies in France, the Netherlands and England and her Atlantic trade routes were threatened. The excessive borrowing Philip resorted to in order to meet these commitments finally forced him to declare his third bankruptcy in 1596. By the time of his death in 1598, he must have well understood the despair that had driven his father to abdicate in 1556.

The 1590s were a difficult decade everywhere in Europe. A 'mini ice age' caused a catastrophic drop in mean temperatures across the continent, and agricultural yields fell to record low levels, forcing up prices and impoverishing the bulk of the population.[1] France, still gripped by civil war, experienced her worst famines of the century and endemic peasant revolts. In England, the government introduced the celebrated Elizabethan Poor Law to mitigate the worst effects of famine, plague and poverty. Plague cut a swathe across Italy as well as Castile. In part these desperate circumstances were a product of the wars ravaging the entire Western coastline of the continent, from the Netherlands to Cadiz, and the effects of war were certainly no worse in Spain than in France, for example.

The burden of 50 years of virtually continuous warfare resulted in the collapse of the Spanish economy. The crushing burden of the *millones* was widely resented, and in many places was never fully collected. Drought affected many parts of the peninsula and poor harvests in 1594, 1597 and 1598 caused famine. In its wake, plague struck several cities, including Santander (1596), Madrid (1598) and virtually the whole of Castile in 1599, killing perhaps 8 per cent of Spain's population. The death rate doubled or trebled across Castile and the population growth of the previous century ground to a halt, although Casey points out that this trend was very patchy, with some towns or areas evading the worst effects of the crisis, principally because they had encouraged the emergence of new crops or industries.[2] Even the Council of Finance joined the chorus exhorting the King to reduce taxes:

> The cities and big towns are empty of people, the smaller villages completely depopulated, the fields with scarcely anyone to till them ... This misery ... comes principally from the burden of taxes and from spending all the proceeds on foreign wars.[3]

Meanwhile, the rest of the empire was suffering, if anything, worse than Spain. Italy, especially the South, endured a 'century of crisis', during which the 1590s were merely a particularly bad decade. Naples experienced a series of disastrous harvests, resulting in famine in 1585 and more or less throughout the 1590s. The vice-regal government issued decrees against food hoarding every year from 1589 to 1593, and then again in 1596. Ration cards were issued and police measures stepped up, in expectation of a repeat of the rioting of 1585. These precautions narrowly averted an anti-Spanish conspiracy in 1599.[4] The steady population growth of the sixteenth century halted in the 1590s, and fell during the following century and demands by the government in Spain for taxation inevitably fell upon deaf ears. Rural communities in particular struggled to meet tax demands, resulting in 'the emigration of many citizens, who could not afford such taxes'.[5] A similar picture emerges in relatively urban, industrial Spanish Lombardy. As the unusually wet winters and dry summers of 1590-1593 forced up grain prices, peasants converged on the major towns in search of work, and this increased upward pressure on prices and downward pressure on wages. In turn high food prices and increased government spending on poor relief and imported emergency supplies of grain depressed demand for manufactured goods, which consequently experienced a trade depression. However, the constant demands of the Netherlands war kept the armaments industry (a Milanese speciality) healthy, as did Milan's role as a staging post for Spanish troops en route to and from the North.

Yet, despite the existence of plague, famine and war, Spain itself was remarkably stable. The popular revolts that shook France during the 1590s were not replicated south of the Pyrenees. In particular, Castile, racked by plague, dearth, war and economic collapse, was extraordinarily passive. There was rumbling dissatisfaction. Street urchins publicly taunted the returning Duke of Medina Sidonia after the Armada disaster, but although this indicates the extent to which the regime's failures undermined traditional social deference, there was no substantial rebellion during the final years of Philip's reign, except the largely aristocratic and highly localised 'Aragonese Rebellion' (see pages 43–5). However, whilst the crisis in Spain was not characterised by widespread social unrest or revolt, the financial, economic and demographic problems experienced in the peninsula were symptomatic of the changing fortunes of Spain. 'The bankruptcy of 1596 meant ... the end of Philip II's imperial dreams.'[6] The government's failure to put right the problems facing Spain in the 1590s was attributed widely to the aged and ailing monarch, whose health often prevented him from engaging in the business of government as energetically as he once had done. One cannot escape the impression that the loyal and long-suffering population of Spain, from the court aristocracy down to the street urchins, was waiting for the 'old man' to die, in the hope of a new era.

2 A Golden Age of Spanish Culture?

> **KEY ISSUE** Was the reign of Philip II a 'Golden Age' of Spanish cultural achievement and greatness?

Although Philip II's reign is often portrayed as a period during which Spain, under the watchful eye of the Inquisition, turned in on itself and fell behind the rest of Europe in artistic and cultural terms, this rather broad-brush judgement does not reflect either the King's attempts to encourage art, architecture and scholarship during his reign, or the vibrancy and variety of Spanish culture under Philip II.

Philip spent much of the decade before becoming King in Flanders, and his visits to Italy during the regency left a deep impression upon him. Consequently, on his return to Spain in 1559, he set about trying to share some of the renaissance culture of his other possessions with Castile. Perhaps the greatest outlet for Philip's

Philip's private palace-monastery of San Lorenzo el Escorial, built at a cost of five million ducats between 1563 and 1585, is regarded as an expression of Philip's dignified, remote and austere monarchical style.

artistic energies was in building. In 1561 Philip moved his capital to Madrid, chosen because of its centrality to the network of Royal palaces in Old Castile. Over the next 25 years, the *Alcazar* (royal citadel) at Madrid was remodelled and extended, a new hunting lodge at El Pardo, just outside Madrid, was constructed and the royal residences at Valsaín in the Segovia Woods and Aranjuez were extensively redesigned and improved. The gardens at Aranjuez were completely redesigned by Flemish gardeners in the fashionable style of Northern Europe. All of this work was closely supervised by the King, who visited the sites regularly and studied and commented on both the builders' plans and the progress reports. His preference for renaissance styles in architecture and garden design was evident in his employment of Juan Batista, who had been with him in Flanders during the 1550s and who brought with him the latest styles and techniques from Italy and the Netherlands. Batista's (and Philip's) greatest project was the construction of San Lorenzo El Escorial, Philip's private monastery, palace and mausoleum in the cool, secluded Guadarrama hills northwest of Madrid. Designed by Batista, largely constructed by his pupil, Juan de Herrera, but personally altered to his tastes by the King, the Escorial was Philip's most impressive enduring legacy, a magnificent, austere and simple construction, in which the King took refuge when he wished privacy to be with his family or to get important work done. It contained a Jeronimite priory, a royal residence, a magnificent chapel and a mausoleum, in which the bodies of Philip's forebears and family were gathered from around Spain and laid to rest. Philip was a frequent visitor to the Escorial, where he felt able to escape the heat and bustle of Madrid and enjoy a few days of contemplation and work undisturbed.

Philip's patronage of architecture did not extend merely to palaces. He took a close interest in the reconstruction of Valladolid after a great fire in 1562. His interest in art extended beyond building too. He brought the Italian artist Titian, whose work he greatly admired, to Spain where he worked at Philip's court for several years, producing a series of portraits and important allegorical works celebrating Philip's achievements and victories in the first half of his reign. Besides a substantial collection of Titian's work, Philip collected more than 1,400 other works by such luminaries as Heironymous Bosch and Antonis Mor. He brought the Italian sculptors Leoni and Pompeio Leoni to Spain, and encouraged Spanish artists, notably the portrait painter Alonso Sanchez Coello. However, he disliked the work of Spain's greatest artist of the era, El Greco, who consequently had to seek patronage outside the Court.

Philip was a less enthusiastic patron of writers, although St Teresa of Avila enjoyed the King's protection throughout her life, despite the accusations that her poetry and writings bordered on the heretical. Philip's education was evident through his patronage of the humanist scholar Arias Montano, who was commissioned to produce a poly-

Titian's 'Religion Succoured by Spain', painted between 1572 and 1575, celebrated the victory of Philip's naval forces over the Turks at the battle of Lepanto in October 1571. The seascape in the background refers to the battle.

glot (multi-lingual) translation of the Bible for scholars, but on the other hand the writings of such humanist greats as Erasmus and St Thomas More were banned, and several Spanish humanists and writers were forced into exile or silence by the attentions of the Inquisition during Philip's reign. Philip's personal thirst for knowledge was legendary. He established a state archive at Simanças and dispatched instructions to regional governors and viceroys to assemble immense questionnaires about their corner of the empire. A scientific expedition was dispatched to the Americas in 1571, and in the same year, the King appointed Juan Lopez de Velasco to map Spain's New World possessions. Velasco's *Geography And Universal Description Of The Indies*, published in 1574, was the outcome. One enduring legacy of the reign was a remarkable collection of cityscapes, drawn for the King by the Flemish artist Anton van der Wyngaerde during a lengthy tour of Spain in the 1560s. The most important of these commissions were gathered together in Philip's enormous library in the Escorial, which included a personal collection of more than 4,000 volumes, some of which were banned works by humanists and renaissance scholars such as Erasmus and Machiavelli. His preferred reading appears to have been religious and devotional works, such as St Teresa's *Life*.

The trouble was that few other Spaniards shared the King's enthusiasm for the artistic culture of Western Europe. A few, cosmopolitan members of the royal circle at court had travelled abroad and acquired broader tastes, but the aristocracy as a whole were no great patrons of the arts, and if they did, displayed rather limited, Spanish and conservative tastes, preferring devotional works or the chivalric romances of the day. The soldier-writer, Cervantes received a degree of Court patronage for his romance *Galatea* but his greatest work, *Don Quixote*, post-dates Philip's reign.

The distribution of royal largesse was insufficient on its own to stimulate a Spanish renaissance to parallel that underway at the same time in Northern Europe and England. In this respect, the traditional picture of Spain as a cultural backwater from the mid sixteenth century remains valid. Nonetheless, a Castilian-language literature began to take root during the era, often associated with a popular revival of piety, exemplified by the mystic poetry of St Teresa of Avila and St John of the Cross, and the lyrical-religious poetry of Fray Luis de Leon. However, apart from El Greco, whose greatness ensured that he thrived despite the withdrawal of royal favour, perhaps the only really new cultural development of 'Golden Age' Spain that did not owe its existence to royal patronage was the appearance, towards the end of the era, of the *picaresque* genre of stories and novels. This found most famous expression in Cervantes's classic *Don Quixote*, published in 1604, six years after Philip's death, although its theme of a misguided knight engaging in a series of ill-considered and disastrous adventures might be seen as an ironic comment on the follies of

Philip's foreign policy. Philip would probably have empathised with the errant knight's words:

> 1 The religious, in peace and quiet, pray Heaven for the well-being of the world; but we soldiers and knights carry out what they pray for, defending it with the strength of our arms and the edge of our swords ... We, therefore, are God's ministers on earth, and the arms by which His jus-
> 5 tice is executed here.[7]

But the author was gently mocking Don Quixote's heroic self-delusion, and the common theme of the picaresque genre of novels, the struggle of the outcast and downtrodden in a Spain beset by difficulties, reflected ill on the Philippine era, and would not have gone down well with the King.

3 Assessment: an Age of Imperial Greatness?

> **KEY ISSUES** How has Philip's reign been viewed by contemporaries and historians? What was his legacy to his son, Philip III?

a) Contemporary Views

Philip II died on 13th September 1598, leaving to his successor a similarly difficult and complex legacy to that which he himself had inherited. Many of Philip's contemporaries were critical of the state of Spain at the end of the reign, the *arbitrista*, Barrientos, bemoaning:

> Our realms defenceless, infested, invaded; the Mediterranean and Atlantic lorded over by the enemy; the Spanish nation worn out, prostrate, discontented and disfavoured; *reputaçion* and honour laid low.[8]

As the glorious triumphs of the first half of Philip's reign had given way to the disasters and trials of the last decade, even the King's most unflinchingly loyal subjects had begun to question their sovereign. Within days of Philip's death one of his military commanders, Don Martin de Padilla, declared that 'men will see what the Spaniards are worth, now that they have a free hand and are no longer subject to a single brain that thought it knew all that could be known, and treated everyone else as a blockhead'.[9]

But Philip was mourned by many too, according to the Venetian ambassador.

> 1 The King is dead ... Although change is usually popular, yet nobles and people, rich and poor, universally show grief ... he was a prince who fought with gold rather than with steel, by his brain rather than his arms. He has acquired more by sitting still, by negotiation, by diplomacy,
> 5 than his father did by his armies and by war. He was one of the richest princes the world has ever seen, yet he has left the revenues of the

kingdom and of the crown burdened with about a million of debts. He owes to his good fortune rather than to the terror of his name the important kingdom of Portugal, with all its territories and treasures; on
10 the other hand he has lost Flanders ... Profoundly religious, he loved peace and quiet. He displayed great calmness, and professed himself unmoved in good or bad fortune alike. He had vast schemes in his head: witness his simultaneous attack on England and France, ... while facing the revolution in Flanders ... On great occasions, in the conduct of
15 wars, in feeding the civil war in France, in the magnificence of his buildings, he never counted the cost; he was no close reckoner, but lavished his gold without a thought; but in small matters, in the government of his household, he was more parsimonious than became his station. He held his desires in absolute control and showed an immutable and unal-
20 terable temper ... No-one ever saw him in a rage, being always patient, phlegmatic, temperate, melancholy. In short, he has left a glorious memory of his royal name, which may serve as an example, not only unto his posterity and his successors, but unto strangers also ...[10]

b) Historians' Views

Historians have not always echoed the Venetian ambassador's generous assessment. Until the twentieth century, 'Black Legend' held a good deal of sway amongst historians, but the sweeping judgements of writers like Watson and Motley have been thoroughly dismantled by more recent studies. Elliott tersely observed that, by 1598, 'Philip had spent all he had, and reduced to misery his kingdom of Castile',[11] but Koenigsberger argued that Philip was no tyrant and monster, although his reign was nonetheless ultimately a failure that sowed the seeds of Spain's later demise as a Great Power:

1 The great plans of his last fifteen years had been checked. But he had fulfilled his original intention of preserving his dominions and defending the Catholic faith wherever he could. The northern provinces were lost, but not yet, he hoped, irrevocably. He had fought off the Turkish
5 threat; he had acquired the crown of Portugal ... and, by his intervention in France, he had perhaps even saved that country from being ruled by a heretic King ... These were great achievements. Yet to attain them he had sacrificed the treasures of the Indies and the blood and property of his Castilian subjects. Philip left Castile with its imperial tradition con-
10 firmed but with an economy unable to bear the strains which this tradition had come to involve.[12]

More sympathetically, Pierson sets Philip's policies, victories and defeats in a contemporary context. He argues that the loss of the Northern provinces of the Netherlands was more than compensated for by the acquisition of Portugal, that Philip successfully preserved Catholicism in the empire and introduced the reforming decrees of the Council of Trent, and that he fought the Ottomans to a standstill.

However, the cost was immense and his commitment to the equitable dispensation of justice throughout his territories was lost along the way. Pierson concludes by restating the view that, whilst 'Philip the Prudent' did not seek war, preferring to govern through peaceful means, his reign finished in turmoil, with an insolvent Spain facing defeat on three fronts. However, whilst accepting that Philip proved intolerant and ideologically blinkered at times, Pierson places this in a contemporary context in order better to appreciate the King's position.

Henry Kamen has attempted the most thorough revision of the 'Black Legend'.[13] Kamen's Philip was no reserved and cool secretary, tied up in his papers and remote from the world, but an emotional, cosmopolitan and lively character. His pursuit of religious unity was motivated, Kamen argues, by his hatred of rebellion, which explains his intolerance of heresy and heretical books. However, Kamen perhaps under-stresses the central role of religion in framing Philip's actions, both private and public. His preparedness to hazard all in the expectation of a timely miracle, as the Armada campaign illustrates, and his readiness to justify undefendable actions, like the judicial executions of several Dutch grandees in 1567–8, reveal the influence of his religious faith at difficult moments.

Geoffrey Parker has reinterpreted Philip II as a somewhat anachronistic figure, an ineffective corporate meddler, unable to delegate to his subordinates and prone to imposing a fixed 'world view' on all discussion of policy. There's a seductive familiarity about Parker's picture of the King filtering out unpalatable news or unmanageable quantities of information by applying preconceived ideas about problems. According to Parker, the King's rigid mindset prevented him from responding flexibly and effectively to changing circumstances. The rapid multiplication of problems towards the end of his reign was the direct result of Philip's attempts to 'micromanage' every aspect of his affairs personally when delegation had already been shown to be more effective. Consequently, Philip led his country into a crisis of foreign and imperial affairs almost entirely of his own making. Although Parker's theme is very much foreign and imperial affairs, his conclusions offer a very modern view of the ultimate failure of the Philippine regime in domestic matters too, but his analysis comes perilously close to a 'Management Consultancy Theory Of History', and like all 'big ideas' it can be overpowering and distorting.[14]

It is unarguable that Philip II died leaving Spain facing a 'crisis of empire'. At war with Dutch rebels and England, facing a France made hostile by Philip's inopportune support for the losing side in the French civil war, weighed down by debt, economic collapse and demographic stagnation, Spain was badly in need of new energy and direction. His people and his ministers alike placed the blame for the deterioration in Spanish fortunes upon the former King, yet opinion is divided amongst historians whether Philip ever really controlled affairs sufficiently to merit such criticism. Kamen argues that 'Philip was never at any time in adequate control of events, or of his kingdoms, or even of his own destiny... He could do little more than play the dice available to him',[15] and this recalls Braudel's assessment that the King, as a mere human being, could not significantly affect the long term structural changes in the economy, agriculture, climate and population that would determine the fate of his country.[16] But other historians are more critical of the monarch, arguing that structural factors cannot in themselves completely explain the relatively rapid decline of Spain after its brief 'Golden Age'. The King himself, as the maker of policy, bears a measure of responsibility for Spain's subsequent decline.

References

1 The 'mini ice age' is explored in an accessible and stimulating way in G. Parker, *Europe in Crisis* (Fontana, 1979), Chapter 1.
2 J. Casey, 'Spain – A Failed Transition' in P. Clark, *The European Crisis of the 1590s* (London, 1985), p. 211.
3 Baltasar de Barrientos, *Discurso al Rey Nuestro Senor del Estado que Tienensus Reynos* (Madrid, 1598, reprinted, Madrid 1990).
4 J. Burke 'Southern Italy in the 1590s', in Clark, *European Crisis of the 1590s*, p. 180.
5 Commune of Terranova, cited in Ibid, p. 180.
6 J.H. Elliott, *Imperial Spain* (Penguin London, 1963), p. 287.
7 M. Cervantes, *Don Quixote* (Penguin, 1950), p. 98.
8 Álamos de Barrientos, 1598, cited in H. Kamen, *Golden Age Spain* (Macmillan, 1988), p. 12.
9 Cited in Pearson, *Philip II* (London, 1975), p. 128.
10 Venetian Ambassador Soranzo, cited in J. C. Davis, *The Pursuit of Power* (Harper, New York, 1970) pp. 120–2.
11 J. H. Elliott, *Europe Divided* (Fontana, 1970), p. 366.
12 H. G. Koenigsberger & G. L. Mosse, *Europe in the Sixteenth Century* (Longman, 1968), p. 272.
13 H. Kamen, *Philip of Spain* (Yale, 1997).
14 See G. Parker, *Philip II* and *The Grand Strategy of Philip II* (Yale, 1998).
15 Kamen, *Philip of Spain*, p. 320.
16 See F. Braudel, *The Mediterranean and the Mediterranean World in the Age of Philip II, Vol II* (Fontana, 1973), pp. 1242–1244.

Summary Diagram
Philip's legacy

Titian   Coelho

Cervantes   Pompeii   El Greco   Aranjuez

Fray Luis
de Leon ——— Literature   Art   Building ——— El Escorial

St Teresa   Acosta

St John
of the ——— Religious   A Cultural Golden   Scientific ——— Velasco
Cross   Scholarship   Age?   Enquiry

Arias Montano   Questionnaire
to the American
Colonies

Maintained   Preserved the
Catholic unity   Empire
of Empire

Achievements

**PHILIP
II'S
LEGACY**

PROBLEMS

Financial   Loss of
collapse (1596   confidence in
Bankruptcy)   Spain?

Economic
Crisis &   Military defeat   Governmental
Decline   by France,   paralysis in
England, Dutch   1590s

The 'crisis of the 1590s'?

Working on Chapter 9

This chapter has examined two principal areas of debate, the crisis of the 1590s and the cultural achievements of Philippine Spain. You should produce brief notes on each of these issues, using the following structure to help you.

1. The Crisis of the 1590s. Economic problems; financial collapse of Spain; military defeat; growth of opposition; criticism of Philip's leadership.
2. 'A Golden Age' of Spanish Culture? The importance of royal patronage; architecture; art; literature; other aspects. How important was religion in Spanish culture during Philip's reign?

Remember that there is a lot of useful material in other chapters to help you address the first of these issues. The Aragonese and Dutch Revolts are dealt with in Chapter 4, the economic and financial problems of Spain are explored in Chapter 6 and the collapse of Philip's foreign policy comes into Chapter 8. If you can, glance back at these sections when you are assembling your notes on this issue.

The last section of the chapter brings this book full circle, making a historiographical assessment of Philip's reign (which means an evaluation of the merits of different historians' accounts of Philip's era). Quickly revisit the opening chapter now, and jot down the main strands of each of the main schools of historical thought regarding Philip's Spain. Finally, and this is very important, briefly record your own conclusions regarding Philip's legacy at the end of his reign. Had it been a reign of imperial greatness or a disaster that laid the foundations for the decline of Spain?

Further Reading

Philip II has proved a subject of endless fascination for English-speaking historians over the years, perhaps because he has become, through the Armada, one of the great enemies of English history. Consequently, there is a rich variety of books about Philip II that you can draw upon by way of further reading. You will, therefore, need to be selective about what you choose to read, because there is far more than you will have time to study.

There are many good biographies of the 'Prudent King'. Perhaps the most accessible is **G. Parker**, *Philip II* (Chicago, 1995). This has the virtue of being a good read, by perhaps the most famous and widely read authority on Philip II, and relatively short! Other views of Philip can be obtained from **P. Pierson**, *Philip II Of Spain* (London, 1975) and, more recently, **H. Kamen** *Philip of Spain* (Yale, 1997).

Excellent broad and readable introductions to the era as a whole can be found in **A. W. Lovett**'s *Early Habsburg Spain* (Oxford, 1986), **J. H. Elliott**, *Europe Divided* (Fontana, 1968) and **J. Lynch**, *Spain 1516-1598* (Blackwell, 1991). Also useful are **H. Kamen**, *Spain 1469–1714: A Society Of Conflict* (Longman, 1991), **J. H. Elliott**, *Imperial Spain* (Pelican, 1963) and **A. Dominguez-Ortiz**, *The Golden Age Of Spain* (London, 1971). More directed at a student readership is **G. Woodward**, *Philip II* (Longman, 1992) and **J. Kilsby**, *Spain: Rise And Decline* (Hodder and Stoughton, 1986), which covers the entire sixteenth century in fairly broad-brush terms.

The government of Spain under Philip II has been examined through a series of biographies of some of his most prominent councillors and servants, although gaps still remain. Ruy Gomes is the subject of **J. M. Boyden**'s *The Courtier & The King* (Berkeley, 1975), Alva is sympathetically appraised by **W. S. Maltby**'s *Alba* (Berkeley, 1983), and the controversial Antonio Perez is examined in **G. Marañon**'s *Antonio Perez* (Madrid, 1963). All of these have made important contributions to our understanding of politics at Philip's Court and the workings of faction.

Philip II's religious policies have come under intense scrutiny in recent years, as the debate on the role and importance of the Inquisition in Spain has revived. Largely responsible for this has been **Henry Kamen**, whose recently reissued book *The Spanish Inquisition* (Phoenix, 1997) reignited the debate over the Inquisition and inspired a generation of scholars to revise the history of sixteenth-century Spanish religion. **W. Christian**, *Local Religion In Sixteenth Century Spain* (Princeton, 1981), **A. D. Wright**, *Catholicism And Spanish Society Under The Reign Of Philip II & Philip III* (Lewiston, 1991) and **S. T.**

Nalle, *God In La Mancha: Religious Reform And The People Of Cuenca* (John Hopkins UP, 1992) are worth dipping into for evidence of Catholicism at local level. A useful, although challenging, article on this subject is **H. Rawlings**, 'The New History Of the Spanish Inquisition' in *The Historian* 56 (1997). A restatement of the alternative view that the Inquisition was, after all, an agency of repression and persecution can be found in **W. Makin**, 'The Spanish Inquisition' in *History Review* (March 1997).

Philip II's foreign and imperial policy is very much the domain of **Geoffrey Parker**, whose mastery of the subject is best appreciated through *The Dutch Revolt* (Pelican, 1979). **C. Martin** and **G. Parker**, *The Spanish Armada* (Penguin, 1989) is really only challenged on this subject by **F. Fernandez-Armesto**, *The Spanish Armada* (Oxford, 1988). **G. Parker**, *The Grand Strategy Of Philip II* (Yale, 1998) is a stimulating read, and a structural assessment of the mechanisms by which the empire coped with constant warfare can be gained from **G. Parker**'s *The Army of Flanders & The Spanish Road* (Cambridge, 1972) and **I. A. A. Thompson**'s *War & Government In Habsburg Spain, 1560–1620* (London, 1976) and *War & Society In Habsburg Spain* (Aldershot, 1992). Some useful thoughts on the aims of Philip's foreign policy can be found in **G. Woodward**'s article 'Philip II's Foreign Policy' in *History Review* 21.

Elsewhere, **J. H. Elliott**, *The Old World And The New* (Cambridge, 1970) offers some interesting observations on Spain's relationship with its American colonies, as does **J. H. Parry**, *The Spanish Seaborne Empire* (Hutchinson, 1966).

Philip's problems in the Mediterranean are the subject of one of the greatest works of modern historical scholarship, **Fernand Braudel**'s *The Mediterranean In The Age Of Philip II Vols 1 and 2* (Fontana, 1972–3), which although first written in 1949 remains the cornerstone of much historical thinking regarding Philip's empire. It's very big, but if you dip into it selectively, using the index and the exceptionally detailed list of contents at the beginning, I guarantee you will find something of interest. Fifty years after its publication, it still opens the reader's eyes.

Spain's economic and social history during the early modern era has attracted a number of difficult specialist studies. You could do worse than to read the relevant sections of one or two more general works like Lovett and Lynch, but a useful recent contribution to this area is **J. Casey**, *Early Modern Spain – A Social History* (Routledge, 1999). Also worth dipping into, especially if you want to set the problems Spain experienced towards the end of Philip's reign in a more general European context, is the collection of essays edited by **P. Clark**, *The European Crisis Of The 1590s* (London, 1985).

Sources on Philip II's Spain

The range of published primary sources on the period in English is a little thin, but **J. C. Davis** ed., *The Pursuit Of Power: Venetian Ambassadors' Reports On Turkey, France And Spain In The Age Of Philip II* (Harper, 1970) includes a number of lengthy extracts from the reports of the Venetian representatives in Madrid. There is a small selection of primary sources in **Woodward**'s *Philip II*, and in **K. Leach**, *Sixteenth Century Europe* (Macmillan, 1980).

One exciting source of material is available at the website of Brigham Young University, where you can find a collection of letters from Philip II to his *corregidor* in the *Quatro Villas* (Four Ports) on Spain's northern coast. These are revealing about Philip's style of government, but are available only in summary form in English. The full text is available only in Spanish. The website address is http://www.lib.byu.edu/~rdh/phil2

Index